GO THE DISTANCE

JIM SERGER and JIM SERGER Jr.

GO THE
DISTANCE

A true story of a
father & son's road to recovery

Advantage.

Published by Advantage, Charleston, South Carolina.
Member of Advantage Media Group.

ADVANTAGE is a registered trademark and the Advantage colophon is a trademark of Advantage Media Group, Inc.

Printed in the United States of America.

ISBN: 978-1-59932-285-8
LCCN: 2011940526

This publication is designed to provide accurate and authoritative information in regard to the subject matter covered. It is sold with the understanding that the publisher is not engaged in rendering legal, accounting, or other professional services. If legal advice or other expert assistance is required, the services of a competent professional person should be sought.

Advantage Media Group is proud to be a part of the Tree Neutral® program. Tree Neutral offsets the number of trees consumed in the production and printing of this book by taking proactive steps such as planting trees in direct proportion to the number of trees used to print books. To learn more about Tree Neutral, please visit www.treeneutral.com. To learn more about Advantage's commitment to being a responsible steward of the environment, please visit www.advantagefamily.com/green

Advantage Media Group is a leading publisher of business, motivation, and self-help authors. Do you have a manuscript or book idea that you would like to have considered for publication? Please visit www.amgbook.com or call 1.866.775.1696

THIS BOOK IS DEDICATED TO

ALL PEOPLE WHO NEVER GIVE UP,

AND MAKE DREAMS A REALITY.

Jim Jr. and Sr. tell a powerful story and deserve credit for being so candid as they share both good and difficult memories. In my opinion they have so much to be proud of and this story gives hope to anyone who might be suffering from addiction. The UC Baseball program has produced many success stories - this is as important and inspiring as any of them.

– Brian Cleary
Head Baseball Coach
University of Cincinnati

There are a couple things in life that all people have a hard time dealing with. Two of the most important are the truth, and expressing our emotions. Through Jim taking on this project, I think he found it in himself to accept the past, so there would be a future. In his truthful words we read that by confronting the above obstacles, he's paved a path for his relationship with his dad to sustain.

– Rick A. Wetterau
Long time friend

This book cuts through a quagmire of confusion about the issues of addiction and puts you in contact with a slice of real life. Visions and wholeness in life sometimes come to us in a culmination of suffering and perseverance. Reading this book and digesting its content can make you want to get up in the morning and face the new day with hope and enthusiasm.

– Larry Bechtol
Pastor Matthew United Church of Christ
Cincinnati, Ohio

Truly captivating and genuine. This excellent book takes you on a very personal journey through alcohol addiction in the heart of America. In contrast to many other resources that address addiction, this book is written from the vantage point of a son who provides the reader with profoundly thoughtful guidance about how to raise loving children and build lifelong relationships within our families. I give this read my highest recommendation.

– Dr. Klaus Wagner
MD PhD, Internist and Oncologist
San Francisco, California

Table of Contents

Acknowledgements

PRE-GAME

As I was finishing this book, I went on a walk with my wife and our little girl. We strolled to the pond in the neighborhood, my daughter on her scooter and my wife leading our dog. We went down and skipped a few rocks, then walked over to the playground and began talking to a couple and their two little kids. As I saw my daughter and wife engaging with them in conversation, I realized, *I am a success; I have everything. There is nothing in this world that I can ever have that would be more special than those two meaningful people.*

TO MY WONDERFUL WIFE, TARLA, AND MY LITTLE DOG-LOVER, MY DAUGHTER, MAGGIE:

I love you both with everything I have, and there is not a day that I do not get excited about seeing you both. You both are exactly what I wanted in life, long before I ever got married. I dreamed of having a caring, thoughtful wife – that has come true. I dreamed of having a beautiful daughter – that, too, has come true, for I know our future together will a very special one.

Thank you both for putting up with me through this book and, more importantly, thank you for believing in me through the process. I love you both.

TO MY DAD:

We have achieved another accomplishment in our lives. That accomplishment is having this book published. It was only a dream to you and me, but we made it work. We put our thoughts on paper just like we were talking to each other. I love you and I enjoyed doing this book with you. Thank you for allowing us to become closer than ever before.

TO MY MOM:

Thank you for having the wisdom and the courage to believe in Dad. This book also is living proof that spouses have a pivotal role in the outcome of a loved one. Your strength and your audacity is why our family has kept together for so long, along with your willingness to do whatever it takes to share that love. I love you and respect you for your accomplishments in life and, more importantly, for the love you gave our family and me through all the difficult times. I love you.

TO MY BROTHER:

Thank you for finishing the journey with me as well. I am so glad
that you were the best man at my wedding. I could not have asked
for a better little brother. I hope that you know how much
I love you.

TO MY UNCLE KEN:

Thank you for standing by your brother, and for keeping watch
over him. Your strength and your courage are the greatest assets
a brother could ask for. You should stand up straight with your
shoulders back and head up high, and be proud that you were a
constructive part of why my dad, your brother, is alive and
sober today. I love you.

TO MY DAD'S TWO BEST FRIENDS, PAUL AND DONNY:

Your love of him long ago, your love of him through his hardship,
and your love for him today, defines the word "friendship." Thank
you so much, for standing by my mom, standing by me and, most
importantly, believing that my dad, your friend, was still of value to
you, through the good and the bad. I love you both.

TO THE PROSPECT HOUSE:

Thank you for delivering what your system stands for.

TO THE HALFWAY HOUSE, MOUNT AIRY SHELTER:

Thank you for never giving in and for standing your ground.

TO A.A.:

Wow! What can I say? Your passion for helping an individual to be successful is why your system works.

TO ALL OF OUR FAMILY AND FRIENDS:

Everyone who made this true story come to life, you make my dad and me that much stronger, too. We love every single one of you.

**TO THE FAMILY AND FRIENDS WHO HELPED
ON THIS PROJECT, WE WOULD LIKE TO RECOGNIZE
THEM FOR THEIR INPUT AND SUPPORT
OF THIS BOOK:**

John and Kathy Fuchs, Larry Bechtol, Chris Serger, Lee Ungrund, Eric Schafer, Dori and Klaus Wagner, and Rob Gillum.
Thank you all for helping out and cheering us on.
We love you guys very much.

TO PAT WILLIAMS:

Thank you for being a leader, a great motivational teacher and a true inspiration to my family and me. You make this world a better place.

TO ADVANTAGE MEDIA GROUP:

They have made my first experience a very memorable one. They coached me through all the steps, they guided me through all the editing and they are a great group of people and I would recommend them to anyone. Brooke White, Alison Morse, Jenny Tripp, Kim Hall and the rest of the corporation – Adam Witty should be a very proud person knowing that he has a great staff on his hands, one which represents his mission statement to a T.

1ST INNING

"YOU CAN DISCOVER MORE
ABOUT A PERSON IN AN HOUR OF PLAY,
THAN IN A YEAR OF CONVERSATION."
– Plato

LET'S PLAY CATCH

Naturally I cannot remember the day I was born. No one can. All I know of my birth is through photos that my mom and dad have, the stories that they share, and the insights that they talk about. My first memory was when we lived in Louisville, Kentucky. It was a very snowy night, very inviting to a five-year-old, and I kept begging to go out into it. My dad grabbed the old wooden sled with the two metal gliders, and off we went. It was something out of a Christmas card or a Robert Frost poem, as I remember it. Snow everywhere; no one was out, lights were on in the distance and it was like the night was meant for just my dad and me. I remember him running, walking, talking, laughing and joking with me all the way. We were only out about thirty minutes, but I like to think we made a lap around the Indianapolis 500. It felt like it took forever, and that was a good thing. It was a father/son moment that is instilled in my brain forever. Memories of my dad at that age are just as vivid then as they are today at forty. I remember looking at my dad as if he were Superman, Batman, or even the Lone Ranger. Dad was someone whom I looked up to, someone I wanted to be, and someone who other people wanted to be. My dad was a DAD.

As far as a father/son relationship goes, I know for a fact that my father and I had exactly what that relationship was meant to be. It was full of love, it was full of love, and it was full of love. That was it; LOVE. It was caring, sharing wisdom, sharing thoughts and feelings; the openness to reveal our innermost selves, and to consider together the meaning of life.

My dad was not a scholar, psychologist, or a professor. He was a salesman by trade. His dad did it, his dad's dad did it, and so on, and so on. My dad is and always will be a great salesman. He was a salesman 24/7. No matter what the circumstance was, the salesman in him always kicked in. I would come home covered in mud, and he would say "Boy, don't you look great!" Or we would run into an old friend of his and he would say, "Have you lost weight?" No matter where my dad was, he always had kind words for other people. Neighbors, Christmas time, graduations; no matter what the situation or occasion, my dad was a leader. When he walked into the room, everyone seemed to know his name, just like Norm in Cheers. Everywhere he went, people knew him.

My dad's name is James Edward Serger, but the name that fits him best, to me, is Dad. His whole life, he was involved in sports. He played third base at the University of Cincinnati. His mom was Makatiwa Country Club golf champ, and his dad was an avid golfer and a season ticket holder for the Cincinnati Bengals and the Cincinnati Reds. I had many sleepovers at my parents' house with my friends, and every time they were there, Dad would tell us the story of how he hit the game-winning home run that put UC in the running for the College Baseball World Series. The cherry on top of the sundae was that subsequently he was picked by the Philadelphia Phillies. He'd played summer semi-pro baseball, and a Phillies scout had spotted him. I must have heard this story a billion times, but it never got old for me. He didn't accept the offer, because it would have lost him his student deferment and he'd have had to go to Vietnam. Instead, he chose to attend the University of Cincinnati to get his time in.

Wanting the best for his son, Dad put me in an upper baseball league when I was all of six, so that I was playing with kids that were in second grade when I wasn't even in first. We had just moved back to Cincinnati and into a huge subdivision. There must have been 1,000 homes in our new neighborhood, the place where my dad's and my relationship would grow into the special, loving, father/son bond it became. I would make lasting friends in my new league and, together with my parents and my little brother, began a new life in Cincinnati, where we'd be for many years.

The day we moved into our house there, my dad and mom were sitting on the back porch when a young kid came tearing around the corner, and asked them, "Do you have a son?"

Dad told, him, "Yes."

The boy told them that I had been hit in the head with a baseball bat, and that I was lying in a pool of blood. I remember my parents rushing me to the hospital, my dad at the wheel and me lying in the back seat on Mom's lap. I am sure he was flying, because in those days, you didn't call 911. You just drove to the hospital as fast as you could. He was running lights and stop signs to get from the east side of Cincinnati all the way downtown, to make sure that his son was alright. I came out of it fine, though I still have the scar on my forehead. I remember my mom telling the story as if it were yesterday. As far as I was concerned, my dad had a cape on his back. Not really, but to a six-year-old, he sure as heck did.

I was born on February 24, 1971, on Ash Wednesday. I was given the name James Edward Serger, Jr. My dad, a young salesman in Cincinnati, had decided to buy a ton of "It's a Boy!" cigars. Unfortunately for him, it was Lent, the time of year when practicing Christians choose to give something up as a religious observance, and Dad had chosen the one item which it seemed that everyone had given up for Lent. Having bought so many cigars, he could not afford to just throw them away, so he decided to smoke them himself. Cigars turned out to be his trademark. In every picture of my dad, he's got a cigar in his mouth. He didn't smoke the big, huge ones, but little White Owls. Looking through our family picture albums, I came across a photo of him pushing me around on a spinner at the park, with a cigar in his mouth. At the time, it was okay to smoke cigars almost anywhere.

As I grew older and continued to play on sports teams, my dad would even coach us with a cigar in his mouth. Everyone recognized him by that trademark; when players would ask me which man was my dad, I would point at the one with the cigar in his mouth. He was involved in every single aspect of my life as a little boy. He would assist in coaching my teams, and was the head coach of my brother's teams. Baseball was his main sport to coach, but Dad was usually involved in my soccer teams, too, assisting at our practices. When I was in fifth grade, he helped out with the basketball team. Many of my team photos feature Dad in the picture along with me and the other players, always with that cigar. From the time I started first grade at I.H.M. in Cincinnati, I just remember that no matter what the event, my dad was there. Baseball, football, soccer, basketball, homework, PTA meetings, PTO, Boosters, festivals, fund drives – my dad and my mom played active parts in my life. One season when I was in the CYO basketball league, my dad traveled to all ninety games to watch me play. Sometimes that meant three games on Saturday and on Sunday, too. My dad was there. Other fathers attended as well, but my dad made it to every single game. Nine o'clock on school nights, he would be with me. Saturday at eight in the morning, he was there, and Sunday at eleven, he was there, too.

My dad enjoyed watching anything that had to do with the Reds, Notre Dame, UC or the Bengals. In 1980, the Bengals were bound for the Super Bowl, but I was in CYO basketball. Dad never missed my games, even though it meant he missed the Bengals. To this day, he says he would much rather be watching his kids play sports and supporting them, than sitting at home watching the Bengals or anything else. That is how my dad was; there for *ME*, being the father and the leader that I needed him to be at my young age. I hear today of parents not making it to their kids' games, not supporting their schools, not there to lend a hand. That was certainly NOT my parents; they were engaged in every aspect of my young life.

In the 1970s, the interest rate on our home mortgage was fourteen percent. As I recall, my parents bought our two-story house for $48,000 in 1977. Even with pennies being squeezed, I remember that my parents had people over to our house all the time. Every Sunday in the summer, we had a cookout. Grandparents, aunts, uncles, neighbors; it didn't matter how many people came, we were going to feed them and have a good time. Some days, it would be more than forty people over at the house. I guess that in those days, like today, going out was expensive. Getting a keg, dogs, and chips was a ton cheaper, and we found lots of ways to enjoy ourselves. We would play badminton, croquet, or lawn jarts. My parents would tell stories, and so would Grandpa, or even Great-Grandma. It was a slower time. Nobody was ever in a rush to leave, and sometimes I think that my dad would happily have kept the party going until daybreak. He and my mom loved to entertain people. They did not have a ton of money, but I believe that that was their way of paying it forward. Adults and kids from all around the neighborhood would come over. Folks would walk up to our house just to say hello to my family. Everyone knew my parents. Out of the one thousand families in the neighborhood, I would guess seventy-five percent of them knew my parents. My dad hung around with some pretty famous people, and would talk about them as if they were coming over.

No matter whether there was a party on or not, every night Dad would make time to play catch with me out back. It was our special time for each other, and we'd talk over everything, from school to sports to whatever. Some days, it was easy to go out and play catch. Other days it had to be hard on him, coming home after a long day at work, but he was still willing to get up and throw the ball around.

To this day I have a baseball glove with my full name and my parents' old home phone number still written on it. I would guess it cost around $100 back in the late '70s. It still works, and I know that we got our money's worth on that. When my dad bought it, my parents got in rather a heated little argument about the purchase, my mom says, but ultimately she supported my dad's decision, and thirty years later I still have it. That is one heck of a return. If I were a Rawlings baseball glove salesman, I'd take a picture of that glove so that people could see how long one lasts, even when it is used and used and used again. When he gave it to me, I remember us rubbing oil on it all night, squeezing it and squeezing it. Then, we wrapped rubber bands around it and left it in the closet for two days to help form it into a pocket, so I'd be able to use it in the coming season.

My dad was such a funny man, and I often think back on all of the goofy things that we did as I grew up. One moment that I will never, ever forget happened during the big blizzard of 1977. In hilly Cincinnati, getting around in the snow was never easy to begin with; add a coat of ice, and – whammo! –it was a double whammy. There was a little convenience store on Eight Mile Road that was all of a half mile from the house. The Mette family owned the store and our family, just like everyone else, shopped there for all of the last-minute items, or stuff for Saturdays; beer, chips, pop, dogs. Dad had a Chevy Nova; it was light green in color. He decided to take my brother and me down to the store, for what, I have no idea, probably cigars.

I remember that the streets were covered in packed snow that had turned to ice. There was a slight grade on the road leading down to Eight Mile Road. On the way back up the hill, it was a little tough but we made it to the top, with my brother and me in the front seat; no seat belts. We told Dad that there was a huge snowball around the corner, and that we should hit it with the car. He was up for the challenge. As we turned the corner, this huge white ball of snow stood in front of us. With our car going all of ten miles per hour, he hit that ball. We all were expecting the snowball to shatter around the car – but because of the melting and refreezing of the snow, it had become solid ice. Dad put a dent in the front bumper; I think we laughed for the next two days about that ice ball. I don't think that that ball melted for five months. It was rock solid. That was the kind of humor that my dad enjoyed with my brother and me. He was always, always willing to take a chance, to get us kids to laugh and have fun.

When I think of the leaders whom I've known in my life, my favorite leader is my dad. As I've grown older, I respect even more the way in which he led me as a son, as well as his peers in the neighborhood, on the ball field, at school and at church functions. He was always there to lend a hand with anything. At Immaculate

Heart of Mary Grade School, my parents (it seemed) were involved in every aspect of my eight years there. The most vivid memory I have of my dad there was of him working the high/low booth at the annual Catholic festival. Man, was that booth busy – not because it was such a great attraction, but because my mom and dad made it fun. "People persons"—that is what they were. I remember running around the festival with my friends every single summer, and my parents working the high/low booth. I recall going over to the Italian sausage booth, asking Mr. and Mrs. Pieples if they could make me another one. Boy, were they delicious!

People loved that high/low booth, because of the way my dad had of making it seem like so much fun; talking to people, telling them to "ante up," or "don't play that hand"—just making the person on the other side feel like this was the most exciting experience they could be having. That is how my dad was to me; he made every moment of our lives together something of EPIC proportions. It did not have to be expensive, but it was *EPIC*; every experience with him seemed heightened, bigger, and better. And even on the day he ran that high/low booth, I'm sure he'd made time to coach my brother's or my baseball team that morning before the festival started. He was the dad that had the "S" on his chest all the time. I'm sure that other dads must have seemed like heroes to their sons, too, but to me my dad was King Kong, the Big Cheese, the Ultimate Warrior.

Christmas time was a huge deal for our family. I remember that we always put up a real Christmas tree - that was how it had to be. One Christmas, my parents, my brother and I drove way out east to a Christmas tree farm, to take in all the holiday cheer. We had never cut our tree down ourselves before. My folks thought that taking my brother and me would be something different, and it was. I got to carry my dad's chain saw. Now, my dad was no Paul Bunyan. He was no Davy Crockett, either. He was a salesman that got a chain saw for Christmas one year, and that was that. But to see him go out there and cut that tree, was like Clark Griswold doing it with his family; you just had to be there. He cut the tree down, and I got to carry the chain saw back to the car. I flung it over my shoulder, over my brand-new baseball jacket that I'd gotten from the summer team sponsor—and the gas cap fell off, covering me in gasoline and oil.

That did not ruin our day, though, because on the way home we stopped at Gold Star Chili in Ripley, Ohio and we had lunch. Now, every family is weird at moments, and this was one of them. My parents were always reminding my brother and me about the importance of saying "thank you." When the waitress took our order, we said "thank you," when she filled each glass full of water we said "thank you," when she gave us a straw we said "thank you," and it went on and on and on. We were not being rude, but we got to laughing so hard with the waitress that we just could not stop giggling, and it went on through the whole meal. That is how my dad taught us to mind our p's and q's, while at the same time giving us the leeway to be human and be kids.

He was a salesman, so he had to know when to play around and when to be serious. He was a good dad. Not once did he ever hit me as a kid. But one time, he did throw me against the wall. I had thought that I would be cute and trip my brother; Dad found out and said, "Okay, just do not do it again." Then a few weeks later I did do it again. This time, Dad picked me up and threw me against the wall, and said, "Do I have to tell you again?" Of course, he didn't have to, not ever again. He was a kind-hearted man but when he was right, he knew he was right. That moment he was right.

Growing up in a family that loved sports, loved travel, and loved me very much, it was hard for me as a little boy, or even as a teenager, to imagine my dad in any other role than being a dad. He was just "Dad," and that was it. One year, our family decided to go to Michigan for a little family vacation. Dad had just gotten a new company car, a white Chevy Monte Carlo SS. Man, it was cool; we drove up and got to see the lake. At this point in his life, Dad looked like a taller Danny DeVito or Kevin James; he was 5' 11" and around 250 pounds. Looking back, I guess he was totally out of shape, but to a fourteen-year-old? No way – he was Dad!

We had just arrived at the lake when my brother spotted the lifeguard chair. Very excited, he sprinted to it and climbed up. He hadn't been up there more than ten seconds before he began to scream. With that, my dad changed into his superhero costume. He ran to my brother. What had happened was that a large fishing hook had gone through the back of my brother's calf, and out the other side. Now, I did not have a stopwatch that day, but to see my dad in action was amazing. He picked my brother up, tossed him over his shoulder, and ran full speed back to the car. Mom and I scrambled in after them, and Dad peeled out and raced to the hospital to get him taken care of. That was what my dad was like to me – a superhero.

Do superheroes hug and kiss? You are darn right they do! My dad is a hugger and a kisser – I mean, for a dad. To this day, even though I'm forty years old, my dad will hug me and kiss me without any thought to what other people are doing, saying, or might think about this show of emotion. He might be in his underwear and a t-shirt, and if someone he had not seen in a while came to the door, he'd probably give them a warm hug anyway. He is not an emotional man at all, but when it comes to fatherly affection, I would say he is in a league of his own. I remember him coaching all the little kids on the ball field, patting them on their heads, giving them little love slaps on the butt, out of affection. It is a good feeling to get a hit or to score a goal, but it is even a better feeling when your coach gives you a high five and a pat or a hug. It shows you that they are in the moment with you, that they are proud of you, and most importantly, that they are giving you their undivided attention in the moment.

One summer, I was playing in two baseball leagues, the 8th grade CYO (Catholic Youth Organization) and the summer league. I was umpiring as well. My dad made it to every single CYO league game, every Sunday. In the summer, he coached my brother's team full-time, so some Saturdays he could not make it to all of my games. He gave it a few innings when he could, or if the games did not coincide, he would make both games. After the games, he would take me to White Castle to grab a bite to eat, then he or my mom would take me to umpiring. I would umpire a few games on one field, then he or my mom would pick me up afterwards. No cell phones in those days, so they had to trust me to be on my own for half the day, and I trusted them to pick me up. But like my dad said, it was no big deal since he was the equipment manager for all of the summer league teams, and he knew all the coaches. They all knew my last name. I would say that out of the fifty games that I umpired, every coach on both sides knew my dad, and always asked me whether I needed a ride home or offered me a snack or a soda after every game. My dad should have run for governor, mayor or even the President of the United States. When good social skills, good temper, good leadership, good moxie and most of all, good solid affection for people come into the race, it is hard to beat. The human touch— he had it, and he was proud of it.

The Christmas of 2010 was a very exciting time for my wife Tarla and me. Our daughter Maggie was six years old, and able to take in the whole Christmas spirit more than in years past. When kids are one, two, three, or four, it is hard and very overwhelming to handle such a huge holiday as Christmas. Things are moving at the speed of light. Now that she is in kindergarten, she and her friends chatter about all their gifts, Santa, the reindeer, Christmas songs, and all the rest, on the bus to school. When I look at her, I can see myself, and I know that when she's grown she will remember us together on Christmas morning, and the gifts all around. Santa's footprints are on the hardwood floors, where he came down out of the chimney. The cookies are half-eaten, the milk is all gone, and the note she left for him was taken. Mom and Dad are coming down the stairs, seeing her with those big eyes, ready to tackle the gifts, like a linebacker ready to sack the QB. That is how I remember my parents on Christmas morning.

The great thing about Christmas morning at our house was that when it was over, we could relive that moment. My parents had audiotaped the whole morning, without my brother or I even knowing.

Those Christmas mornings were so much fun for all of us. One year, I wanted a pair of Pony high-top shoes and I ended up getting two pairs, one red and one blue. The year I remember the most when it comes to my dad was the year he got his wheelbarrow. Now, it's fair to say that he needed a wheelbarrow, but what was in the barrow was something else; BEER. I believe it was Schlitz or Schaeffer. It did not matter to him; it was just an awesome gift. To this day, thirty years later, I think he still has the wheelbarrow – but the beer is long gone.

In the '70s and the early '80s, collecting beer cans was the "in" thing to do for men and for their sons. My room had shelving about twelve inches below the ceiling all the way around, and beer cans were on the shelves. Not just any beer cans, but Cincinnati Reds World Series cans, Billy Beer, Iron City, Steelers Super Bowl cans,

Hamm's, Schaeffer, old pull-top cans, old twist-top cans. Nearly all the cans were tin, and a few were aluminum. It was so awesome to collect those cans with my dad. He would go on business trips and he would come back with two or three new cans that we did not have. He would have people over for Bengal's Super Bowl, or playoff games, or any other occasion that required beer, and he would purchase twenty-four packs of cans that we did not have in our collection. As I said, beer can collecting was the "in" thing to do, and a lot of my friends collected beer cans. Like collecting baseball cards, it seemed very patriotic to collect beer cans. It was a way for my father to share with me all the places he had traveled to, through the different varieties of cans he brought me. It was the same idea as collecting Hard Rock Café shot glasses is today.

With both my dad and I being avid baseball fans, we shared a lot of things, looking back, that were very enjoyable to him and me. The number one thing to me was just being with him. I loved and felt loved by him all the time. We would go to King's Island, Coney Island, the Reds game, the circus or just have a catch together. It seemed like sports were the background for a lot of great talks about school, baseball, football, basketball; everything in our lives together was intertwined with sports. As I write this, it just seems like it was only yesterday that we were out back of his dad's house, playing catch. No matter what, sports were the expression of our relationship, and it's still true today.

As a little boy of ten years old, you see your DAD as a DAD. That was how I saw him; nothing could change my view of him. I loved him for who he was. Coach, father, it did not matter. He was my buddy and we did everything together.

When I was in eighth grade we did not have physical education at my grade school, so we were bused over to the public school so that we could get one hour of physical education with their gym teacher. One day on the way back, as the bus made a right turn, I yelled to everyone on the bus to shift over to the left hand side, and all the students went over to the left. Now, when you're taking a right turn with a bus, you need the weight to be centered and it was not. Low and behold, the bus felt like it was going to flip. At the moment it had seemed like a funny idea, but getting off the bus was a whole different story. Off to the principal's office I went, and principal detention I got. That meant I had to be at school at seven in the morning, one hour before school started.

I'd be in big trouble, I thought, when I got home. Sure, my parents were let down and little upset. But no yelling and screaming; they just talked to me, and my dad said he would take me in the morning. So, off we went the next day at six A.M. Now, I knew that it only took five minutes to get to school. Why were we leaving so early? Good question – my dad took us to Dunkin' Donuts for breakfast, to have the father/son talk. It was great—donuts before school and spending time with him. It worked out for the best, because he was an understanding dad. He did not really care about the school bus incident. What he did care about was the fact that I could have hurt other people, and that was the topic of the meeting. Putting other people's lives at stake and jeopardizing their health was not a good thing to do. I never did it again.

My dad was a dad's dad, he was a friend's friend, and he was what I would consider the ultimate father. He worked hard at his job, he coached two baseball teams in the summer, he put his kids first, and he was always there for his wife and his family. He had a ton of friends, close cousins, aunts and uncles. He had great relationships with his brothers, and with his own father, too. My dad had a great mom as well; Helene Glass Serger. She was a spitfire – or a "fireball," as my dad would describe her. She died of breast cancer at the age of fifty-five. She was the missing link for my dad, as a young man growing up with a wife and two sons. Grandma was always at our games, even when she was bald, and had a wig on to hide her chemo from everyone. She knew the importance of supporting her son and his family and she would do whatever it took to be there. My dad and she were very close, and she was a loving and good-natured person as I remember. Losing a mother so early in life has got to be hard on the oldest son. For my dad it was, considering he was only thirty-four. I believe that losing a close relative at such a young age can make some stronger, but in my dad's case, it made him weaker.

For every bad break or missed opportunity that my dad may have had in his life, there was one thing that I know made him stronger, and that was his family; always there by his side, always there to support him in a new job, always there to support what he would like to do. He is not flashy. I believe just last year his Members Only jacket finally ripped, and the jacket is now hanging in the ceiling of some office building with "SERGER" on the back. He is not one to go out and get a Porsche or an H3, not one to buy new golf clubs, but he would buy his suits from Jos. A. Bank, if he could afford to. He loves to look good and that glow he gives off communicates itself to others. He is the kind of man who turns heads when he walks into a room, without him even noticing why. He will say "hello" first, he will initiate the handshake, and he will give you a bear hug first. He is the instigator, but that is the salesman in him. Looking back, my dad should have been a head coach or a gym teacher instead of a salesman. But in those days, when he was growing up in the '60s, fathers told their sons what they were going to be.

Dad told me a story once about how his father invited three of his business clients to go and watch my dad play baseball. Having his father and his friends at the game made my dad nervous, for he always felt pressured to meet his dad's expectations.

Well, he struck out three times that game and, boy, was he embarrassed with himself. He met his dad's clients and everything seemed normal. But as he climbed into the back of the car to go home with his dad, Grandpa turned around and said very loudly, "Do not ever embarrass me in front of any of my friends again." *Wow*, who was watching out for whom? That is how it was for my dad, always trying to live up to his dad's expectations, instead of just trying to be happy with who he was.

I looked at my dad as a big goof sometimes, and that was a good thing, I viewed our family as a little goofy, and that too was a good thing. My dad would do the dishes every night and play his *Kingston Trio* albums while he cleaned up the kitchen. We ate as a family together for as long as I can remember, all the way up until, I guess, I was eighteen years old. With my brother and me in sports, it did not happen all the time, but five days a week we would eat as a family, at the table with a home-cooked meal. One day, my dad came home from a business trip in New England and with him came two boxes of live Maine lobsters. It was the coolest thing I had ever seen! We put them on the floor and watched them walk around the kitchen, and even better was the way they tasted. But the most enjoyable moment was that it was a goofy moment from my dad to us all. It was a side of him that we saw all the time, happy and cheerful. That is the dad I remember growing up as a kid; always on the fly, willing to go against the stream with our family.

I remember that my dad had quite a few different jobs when I was a kid getting ready to go into high school. I would venture to say that he had around ten before my fourteenth birthday. Some lasted for a few years; others lasted for a few months. He never seemed to be quite happy with what he had, so he always had to get something bigger. For us kids it seemed okay, because you never truly think about your dad's job until you are old enough to understand what a job is. To me, he had a job and that was good enough. His most important job was to be my dad, to be my coach, to be my buddy.

He was one heck of a dad. I had all the perks as a kid, just like all the rest of my buddies. I remember one big day when my parents got our first VHS player. My friend Mark was over, and he, Dad and I went up to the movie rental place and got to pick out our first rental. I choose *48 Hours* with Eddie Murphy; awesome. Needless to say, that choice went over well with the three guys. But when we put it in and began watching with Mom, the video came to a halt real fast. Cuss words like I had never heard before in my life came through the speakers like Frank Sinatra singing *Anchors Aweigh*. A sailor's tone it definitely had. We got really salty fast, but Dad and my mom did not put up with that, so we stopped it. But for him to let me be first one to pick out the video to rent was how my dad was with my brother and me. We could make the choice for ourselves, and he would support our choice, and be willing even to get into a little trouble at home with Mom. But he had learned from his dad's mistakes. He learned the importance of giving kids a fair chance to make decisions on their own, and he did. Just sometimes, the choices were not well thought out.

One job that my dad had was as a bartender at the Mount Washington Bowling Lanes. Oh, that was awesome! We would go see him at work and bowl for free; we would get five dollars in quarters to play the video games. Now, this was a night job, and it was as if Dad was two different guys. One went to work with a suit and tie on, while the other was in a golf shirt. It was natural for Dad to know everyone; everyone in the bowling alley knew him even before he got the job there. Bowling was the "in" thing to do at the time, and video games were the "in" thing to do for kids. With the high interest rates for the homes back then at 13% -18%, going to the bowling alley was a cheap night out for the family. We did not have Atari yet, so going to knock down a few pins was fun for us. But that was not why Dad had the job; he had the job to supplement his income. He was between jobs again and this would be a way to earn a few bucks before he landed a secure job. The whole time I had thought that my dad had two jobs, but in reality he was just interviewing. Giving the impression to his sons that he had a day time job was something he did to keep us from worrying. Then again, at that age I was only worried about friends, sports, bowling, or video games.

As I started writing this chapter of the book I was torn between what I felt I needed to share and what I felt people need to know. The truth is, writing this book has nothing to do with how I feel, or how my dad feels. What is important about my thoughts is how my dad is remembered throughout my life and others that he has impacted. Sometimes, people go through life thinking only about what it should have been. But this book is about what has been and will be forever edged in my dad's and my thoughts of one another. For today – at the age of forty – I see my dad as Dad. That is it. No regrets; I wouldn't change anything about him or me. Our lives have been engulfed in flames, and they have been engulfed in cheers. As I will explain later, our relationship, father and son, is about memories, and that is what we have. Believe me, we have many, many memories still to come in this book and beyond this book.

This book is a challenge that I felt we had to share together, to show that our relationship was still holding strong after so many years. Why can't everyone else's relationships hold true to that statement? The reason is choice. That is it, you make a choice to live on, or you make a choice to die. In the movie *Shawshank Redemption*, Andy Dufran states, "You either get busy living or get busy dying." Which one did my dad choose? The answer is living.

We chose each path that led us to where we are now, and both paths have crossed many miles, some less traveled but some more. And as I go into another saga of our relationship looking back, think of this for a minute before you turn the page. What memories do you have of your mom or dad that are still strong in your memory? Is it all good, or is it all bad? Take the time to play catch; those catches define my memory of my dad as he was to his little boy.

2ND INNING

"ANY MAN CAN BE A FATHER, BUT IT TAKES
A SPECIAL PERSON TO BE A DAD."
– Anonymous

THANKS FOR WAITING UP

I played football in eighth grade and all the way through high school, and there's something to be said for doing that. Football was my passion. Most of us find an extracurricular activity that we love to do beyond the norm, and football was that activity for me. Baseball was my dad's passion, but maybe it was because he did not play football that made football all that much more exciting to him and me. My brother played all the way through high school as well. If there's one important quality to successful fatherhood, that is the ability to support your kids in whatever path they may choose outside of one parent's dreams or hopes. That is what my dad did; support, encourage, and love me.

As you get older and wiser, you also begin to see more clearly the shape of your life. You begin to see how things come together, how life is about responsibilities, about highs and lows, and about money. You see things in a grown-up way. Time and the things that happen to you as you go through grade school change you for the better, for they transform a person from a little innocent child to an adult who has a beating heart and a voice.

That is what happened to me. When you are twelve, you are twelve. But when you hit thirteen – wow! – you're a teenager, a thinker, and you begin to soak in the atmosphere that is surrounding you. My eighth grade year, my parents took my brother and me to Walt Disney World in Orlando, Florida for what I think was our last family vacation together. It was not meant to be that way, but it seems to have been, looking back. We took my dad's company car, a green compact station wagon, all the way down. The Griswolds were off, and yes, there was a U-Haul luggage container on the roof. We went to Saint Petersburg first for a few days, and then on to Orlando from there. This was a great trip for our family. We really had the times of our lives.

In the final week of my eighth grade year, I was playing baseball for the CYO league runner-up game. I was the pitcher for the team. We played all the way over on the west side of Cincinnati, at Haubner Field in White Oak. On the way there I was so nervous, but my dad was with me, and he explained that this was where he'd played semi-pro baseball. It made me feel better, knowing that my dad had also played ball on the same field. Psychologists believe that people are connected from one generation to the next, and by my dad connecting with me through baseball, it was as if I suddenly knew that everything was going to be all right that day. It turned out that we did just fine as a team; we won the game. Dad told a funny story about the park in his day. The team he was on once traded a player to another team for a case of beer. Beer! Twenty-four cans, how small a price is that? Beer was a part of the times in the '60s, '70s, and early '80s, and my dad was right in the thick of it.

Our family lived in Anderson Township, which is on the east side of Cincinnati, and right down from the house was the Ohio River, maybe a mile or two south of where we lived. Just on the other side was the Bluegrass State, Kentucky. I never really understood why we drove to Kentucky on Saturdays as a kid, but as a teenager I began to get the point. BEER. Cheap BEER. Dad could get any beer in Kentucky for two dollars or even five dollars cheaper than he could get it for in Cincy. We drove over a lot when I was a kid, two or three times a month to load up on beer, cigars, and cigarettes for my mom. But hey, to save a few bucks, who wouldn't drive two miles over the bridge to save money? I know I would go out of my way to save a few bucks.

One day, on one of those drives with Dad and my brother over to Kentucky, the topic of the birds and the bees came up. Without any hesitation whatsoever, Dad jumped right into the question. He explained everything to us, all the way there and all the way back. I remember that the radio was playing a commercial for Car X man, and to diffuse the embarrassment of the topic, we began to sing along with the song, "Don't worry, call the Car X buddy!" We began to change the lyrics; "Don't worry, call your grandma!", or "Don't worry, call your mom!" To this day I remember that song, a catchy tune, as my brother would put it. Going to Kentucky was a fun thing to do, because it was like going for a Sunday drive, or driving around and looking at Christmas lights. It was a bonding experience with Dad. It didn't happen often, but Dad would occasionally come back from these trips with a beer in between his legs, sipping it all the way home. Not downing one after another, but just like I would drink a Diet Coke or water, something to wet the whistle.

Lifting weights my eighth grade year was something that would last a long time with me. In 1984 the movie *The Terminator*, with Arnold Schwarzenegger, came out. *Conan the Barbarian, Raw Deal,* all of his movies made me want to be like him; huge. I am now 5'10", but when you are a freshman, you always believe that you'll eventually be 6'2" or 3". I made the JV football team as a freshman. But I took a step down once I made the team, so that I could play with the freshman class. I don't remember why I did that, but as I look back I know that I made the right decision. Making new friends was better than saying "Hey, look at me!"

I had a great freshman year and I loved being at McNicholas High School. My dad had gone there, as had his two brothers. I had one teacher, Bill Fanning, who had also taught my dad years before. Mr. Fanning was an awesome individual, because he was full of life and would tell great stories.

Arnold Schwarzenegger was all I wanted to be in high school; I was going to be the next *Terminator* – and then came Brian Bosworth. He too was a great athlete who I was trying to emulate. I was a pitcher on the JV team my freshman year, and one thing that pitchers *shouldn't* do is lift weights. My dad and I only had a few talks about it, but he was supportive and allowed me to be me. I was never really interested in being a pro baseball player like he was. I wanted to be a pro football player, but at 5"10" and 200 pounds, I knew that shot would not come unless I lifted weights and, boy, did I ever work at it! Freshman year and doing two-a-days with the seniors, I looked up to twin brothers Mike and Mark Browning. I wanted to be just like them. They were always in the weight room pumping iron, encouraging me to do the same, and taking the time to explain to me the benefits. That was the start to my interest in lifting weights.

High school was a great experience for me and for my dad. My dad was just as involved in my life as he was involved in my high school. He was selected to the Boosters Club my freshman year and stayed on until I graduated. As always, I knew my dad was there for me. Not once did he or my mom miss Parent/ Teacher night. They were nearly always involved in any adult functions going on at school. My mom was the first one to get the Spirit Shop off the ground and running, and she would be in school every Wednesday all year around, selling school sweatshirts, blankets, and seat cushions. You name it, she would sell it. My folks were a big part of my life throughout school, and I believe that is why I had a great experience in high school. Those four short years were some of the best times of my life. Our family, no matter what was going on, still had time to eat as a family four or five times a week, even now that my brother and I were in high school. But during the winter break from team sports, I began to take notice of how Mom and Dad always seemed to have private conversations right before dinner. Those talks took place during what was labeled cocktail hour, right in our kitchen, over a scotch and water or a Hudy Delight beer. No matter what, when Dad and Mom were home after work, it was cocktail hour; just a few drinks, no more. But it happened every night. I guess those Kentucky runs really paid off.

The weekends were a different story. It seemed as though we were always going out on the town. I had my friends and they had theirs. My friends' parents became their friends and they still had their family, and their own youthful friends in their circle, too. Friday night and Saturday night were meant for socializing, and my parents did it well. Sometimes when I came home late on a Saturday night, my parents would still be out. Now they were not out and about at bars or at lounges, but they were always out or having friends over to socialize. It was good for them, and for my brother and me, who got to know a lot of people this way. But what was transforming my family was a way of life for my dad that was growing and growing, at a rate that he was unable to stop – and that life revolved around drinking.

My Dad had become President of the school board my senior year of high school. My dad! Mister Baseball himself was now on the education side of the spectrum instead of on the athletic side. I was a below-average C-D student, but in my parents' eyes, that was not good enough, so ultimately I think I graduated with a 2.0 – or straight C's. I was in the lowest level of classes that the school had to offer, and in those classes were all my buddies, from freshman year all the way to senior year; nothing changed. So my dad took it upon himself to challenge me without me even knowing it. On the first day of school after Christmas break, my first two classes were the same with all the same classmates, but third period was a different story. I walked in and there were all of the advanced placement kids and me in the same classroom. I told the teacher that I believed there was a mistake, and she replied, "No, you sit right here in front of my desk."

I looked around. No one was laughing, no one was asleep, and all eyes were to the front. I was not used to this – kids who were smart, that is. I finished that course with the best experience of my education. It was my dad's idea that all kids are smart if you surround them with the right atmosphere, and he did that with me. His point was well taken. Being with the smart kids challenged me indirectly, in that I did not want to be the only student who did not read the book, or the only one who failed the quiz. I got a C in that class – but that was an AP class, not the bottom of the barrel that I was used to. My dad never pushed me to get good grades, for his father had yelled and screamed at him to achieve good grades and he was not about to do that to his sons. But he would challenge us in other avenues to make us better.

It was 1987, and it was going to be one heck of a night to remember for my dad, for it was his 40th birthday party that night.

My mom took him out to dinner and while they were gone, all the family and all his friends came over to the house to get the party started. Kegs of beer, liquor – you name it, and I am sure that we had it. There were at least fifty of his closest friends and family that came over to celebrate Dad's birthday. It was a great time; cheese balls, pepperoni slices, spinach dip, every hors d'oeuvre you could want. My parents loved to entertain, and the party went off without a hitch and everyone had a great time celebrating his birthday. But it was not just a birthday, it was a social event. Now, as an adult, I know why my parents were in the social business. Shoot, who could afford to go and paint the town red, when the interest alone on our house payments was enough to buy a car in those days? If everyone invited to the party was to bring one item, then all fifty people could enjoy the festivities without spending a lot of money. That is how my parents were able to face the high rates in the '70s and early '80s. Plus, back then, families were much tighter than they are today. Every event was a big event. Not just one or two couples, but the whole neighborhood would come over. We would spend a lot of Fridays and Saturdays going over to my parents' friends' house. Paul and Marcia were Mom and Dad's two best friends. They had two girls close to the same age as my brother and me, and the grownups would stay there till three or four A.M., playing cards.

As one gets a little older, the real world begins to take shape, and without even knowing what the problem was, I had sensed that my parents were not doing very well. I never really knew for sure what was going on, but my dad had what I realized were a lot of jobs. Not bad jobs, but salesman jobs and that just never could hold true for my dad. "This job," whatever the newest one was, was always going to be the big one; he would leave for a week and come back with an awesome new company car, like that white Monte Carlo SS. Then, within six months to a year, it would be gone and he'd be off to another job. The whole process would take shape again; six months, then land another job, or maybe one year, land another job.

The one thing that was great about my dad not having a steady job was that he was able to be so involved in my life. My senior year at homecoming, I drove to school to get ready for the game. My date was nominated for Homecoming Queen. My parents realized that she did not have her flower on, so my dad took it upon himself to drive all the way back to school to get the flower, so that she could have it on when her name was called. My dad drove all the way back. I had to say it twice, because although it was not a big deal for him, it was a big deal for my date. He and Mom made sure that she had a flower on, so that she was able to look and feel her best. It was good as a young man not to have a dad with a high-stress job, but his not having a steady, solid job was to be of some concern the older I got.

My dad is and was a huge sports fan, a coach, a mentor and a team player. He could stand all by himself at a football game watching me play, and before he knew it, twenty or so other parents were sitting next to him chitchatting. It drove him crazy. He loved people, but he loved watching my brother and me play even more. His game face would be on; his eyes were locked on the play for the whole game. It was not a social event to him, it was a game, and he was in it from start to finish. He would be in the stands with his cigar in his mouth and just root and holler all game for me and for the team, supporting me. One of my favorites memories about my dad was how, after all of the football games, my friends and I would go out until twelve or so, then I'd head back home. I would unlock the door, and downstairs in the family room I'd find my dad, wide-awake. He'd have a beer on the table; not drunk, but just smoking his cigar and waiting to talk to me about the game. We would talk about what high school team won and which ones lost. I made the news once in football, and he was waiting up to tell me all about it. He wanted to hear what I had to say about the game, and more important he wanted to tell me what a great game I had played. I may have had a lousy game, but he never looked at it that way. He always gave me a hug and told me how proud he was of me. That was the relationship my father and I had. We would hug, and even give each other a kiss.

He and I were the ideal father-son combo that you read about and you want others to have. We had each other's backs. He told me that if anyone had ever hurt me, he'd have killed him. It never came up with dad getting ready to throw down with another parent, but I know that he meant it. I know that if someone had injured me, Dad would have done his best to take care of the situation as a leader first, then as a parent second. He was the line leader all the way through high school with other parents. We could be in the mall and other fathers would walk out of their ways to shake his hand. He was no celebrity, no famous athlete; he was my dad. He was the kind of person who would instigate a conversation with a complete stranger, just to make the other guy feel comfortable. He was a social giant, and still is.

My junior year of high school was the first time that I had a real job. Gold Circle Department Store was my first go 'round. I was seventeen years old, and got the job two weeks before Christmas. My fifteen-year-old brother also got a job, at Convenient Food Mart next to our house, that same year. I had always had jobs in the summer months in high school, cutting grass; I was even the lawn caretaker for the next-door neighbors for one summer. I got my green thumb there. A job was a great thing for me because I loved to work, so Gold Circle was the place for me over the holidays. I worked there all of forty-five days. It was fun, but then my brother got me a job at Convenient Food Mart. This little store was not really all that small, since it did a million in sales in 1988 and still continued to prosper in the '90s. The store was in a strip mall with Dominos Pizza, Cincinnati Federal Savings and Loan, and Summit Meats. It was here at the store that my dad was to make the biggest impression on my life, for the store was surrounded by a thousand homes and in the neighborhood where everyone knew my dad. I met more people working at that convenience store than I had ever thought I could get to know. "You're Jim Serger's son," "You're little Jimmy;" it went on all the time.

I was the cashier, and my brother was the bottle boy. We worked together for three years, and we had a ton of fun. We loved the managers of the store, Kevin and Brian, but the owner, their dad Earl, was out of this world. He ran the store for my first two years. Then he turned it over to his two sons to run. My dad and mom would come in all the time to buy items. Some items I think were bought just so that they could see their sons hard at work. "Hard at work," it is funny for me to apply that phrase to working for Earl, because he was the first mentor I had, beyond my dad and my coaches, who really took a loving interest in me. My dad had faith that Earl would see to it that his two sons were taught the value of a hard day's work, and Earl did that. He was the mentor, the leader, the mortar of the store. When I was just seventeen, Earl gave me the responsibility of ordering all of the store's groceries. But when the truck came in, Earl realized I had doubled up on every order. He did not care at all. We just had to build a few more displays to get rid of it faster. My dad would come in after work to see how I was doing and buy beer, chips and cigars, or whatever he needed for that night. I would sneak him a free soft-serve ice cream just for stopping by to see me. Convenient Food Mart became a part of my family's life for a good four years, from seventeen to twenty-one for me, and fourteen to eighteen for my brother. We made so many new friends working there that it became the social hangout for us even on days when we weren't working.

3RD INNING

"THE GREATEST GIFT I EVER HAD
CAME FROM GOD; I CALL HIM DAD!"
– Author unknown

A GAME CHANGER

High school, getting a driver's license, dating – those were the things that being sixteen to eighteen was all about. But seeing your parents argue was not a good thing at that age. When I say argue, I mean loud talks; there were no "I hate you's" or bad language thrown out at each other as far as I remember, but seeing your parents argue is no fun. But it was for the best; my mom finally had to take a stand on my dad's jobs. My dad was a dreamer. Having dreams is what life is all about. Giving yourself tangible goals, having a to-do list, those things are great – but that was not my dad.

Walt Disney was a dream maker, but he was practical in his creativity, in that he knew just dreaming something up would not create his outcome. My dad, on the other hand, was a dreamer who always believed that the next job would be his biggest job ever. Having talked with him about jobs and responsibilities, I see through his experience the value of remaining at the same job and advancing, instead of job jumping as he did. There is nothing wrong with creating more opportunities for one's own gain, but when a family is involved, job jumping is not a fun game to play. Climbing the corporate ladder, I think, is more challenging that just hopping on the next train bound for another new company. My dad's experiences have shown me that sticking it out in one job is much better than always searching for the next new one. He never really showed any care for whatever job he had; he was so busy looking for the next big stage that he forgot what it is like to live in the present and to be content with what is in hand now.

Jobs; they are a funny notion applied to my dad, because with a job comes responsibility. This was a huge word for my dad to overcome, and he never did, as I saw it. There was no set schedule for my dad to follow. Yes, he had to be at work, but no set time; he was in sales. 10 A.M., 11 A.M., 1 P.M. – these were meeting times that were set up for him, not a nine-to-five job. This avenue was the poorest that he could have chosen, because it took real time management skills to balance a day full of meaningful little jobs, and back then a "liquid lunch" was without a doubt still seen as socially accepted. Taking a customer out to lunch and having two or three drinks was seen as the thing to do. Some people do that today. You may think it is cool or funny to order a drink at lunch, but all we are doing is hurting ourselves, and possibly the outcome of the meeting. Drinking a beer before 5 P.M. on a school night, what are you thinking? Or more important, where are you going with this routine? *Nowhere.* It's like being on a payphone after dark; it's no good. My dad needed structure to his work ethic.

My dad landed some huge accounts in his day, but for every one he landed there were a ton more that he never got, or just let slip away due to lack of effort. He worked in the paper business, and the plastic business. He worked for Mead Corporation in the Chatfield Paper division and a few other paper companies in the

1970s. In 1981, he left the paper company and worked for two companies that sold custom, injection-molded plastics and plastic bottles – very high profile customers: Procter and Gamble, Andrew Jergens, GE, 3M, STP and others. Working in the '70s and '80s there was a ton of entertaining and traveling involved. All through the '80s and '90s, Dad remained in the paper/packaging business – but his habits were still the same, even though society was changing. Liquid lunches were on the way out, entertaining customers and getting tax write-offs were gone, as was taking customers to games, night clubs and anything else on corporate credit cards. However, Dad was not changing. He would rather lose a job due to alcohol, than land another contract with a customer. He saw sitting at the bar and talking as more important that making a few calls to clients, which cost him more than a few jobs. Then it would start all over again – new job, new company car, traveling – like a broken record.

Through all of these job changes, nobody was really aware of my dad's alcoholism. He appeared healthy, happy, intelligent, friendly, charming – and the list went on. He has a great sense of humor, and businesses were willing to hire him and take a chance on him. "This guy will work out," they'd say, "look at his work background. He has everything." Dad did not believe at the time that he was powerless over alcohol – or anything else.

Dad would go to work and, yes, he would come home. But for months that would be all that he did. I would hear my parents in the other room. My brother Andy and I would turn the TV down to try and listen to what was going on. Of course, they always knew what we were doing, so they would talk more softly, and then we would just turn the TV right back up. My dad is, was, has been a great dad, but he was a terrible planner when it came to his own life. That sounds harsh, but he really was. He was so focused on everything else – me, my brother, Booster Club, coaching – that he lost sight of how to focus on himself. He never exercised, never challenged himself as an individual as far as I could tell, but he claims he gave all the attention to the family. What he meant to say was that he was dreaming his life away. John Lennon had that line in a song; "dreaming my life away." Well John Lennon, was doing something about it and he could afford to dream his life away if he wanted to. Money was the root of all my dad's problems when I was in high school. Drinking was just second nature to him. Instead of focusing on his needs as a provider and dreaming about the next, better job, he should have just been happy with what he had, bringing home little bacon strips, instead of a whole pig like he thought he had to. Pressure from one's parents can have a long-term effect on an adult, and I believe that this is what transpired with my dad. His dad was very successful in business, and my dad was trying his whole career to live up to his dad's expectations. But seriously – *who cares?* When a person dies and the hearse is driving down the street, nobody looks for the luggage rack on top, loaded up with all the things the person owned. Do you? I read that line in the book, *A Lifetime of Success*, by Pat Williams.

The best advice that I could give my dad, had I been his best friend, is this: twenty years from now who is going to remember the big contract you got? You will... and that is it. People will remember you twenty years from today as they see fit. Let that be that. First, you were a good father – and he was. Second, you were a good spouse – and he was. Third, you took care of yourself. *And he didn't.*

We lived our lives in the moments surrounding my dad's business. He once took a job in Detroit. Mom and Dad thought we were going to move there, and we did not, although he was still telling her that he had the job. Months passed, and finally she called the business to see what he was doing. They explained to her that he had not worked there in a few months. For two months, Dad was living a lie in Detroit, when he should have just come clean and admitted that he'd lost the job. But he never did until it was too late to do something about it. *Who cares!?* So you lost your job, big deal. There are things in life a lot worse than losing your job, but that is how it was in our lives growing up and all the way through high school. Dad had to fulfill his dreams, at the cost of our family. It was very selfish, and that is where it all started to go wrong in our relationship for the next few years. Instead of thanking him for waiting up for me after the football game, I began to resent the fact that he was hurting my mom. A transformation of his and my relationship would turn it 180 degrees in the wrong direction, a little each day before I graduated high school.

The one person in my life whom I'd always wanted to be like was beginning to become someone that I did not want to be. Little stresses began to show in our relationship. We still made time to play catch in the back yard every once in a while, and he still stayed up to wait for me, so that we could talk about whatever event I'd just come from. But, seeing my mom in the shape that she was in was just not fun at all. For years, my parents had been the ultimate couple to me. Always there, they were always willing to pick me up from practice, or to take me out to get me a new coat for a dance that I was going to. No matter the occasion, my mom was still there for me. My dad was showing his support for me as well, but I began to start to slide further over to my mom's side, the older that I got. It was not that I did not love my dad. I did. I just saw in him someone that was beginning to sink deeper and deeper into a black hole.

My senior year was a great year for me, since I was going to go off to play football in college. I had narrowed my choices down to either Georgetown University in Kentucky, or Wilmington College in Ohio. On both official visits my parents came with me, and we sat in the coaches' offices and heard what they had to say. We watched videos of me on the TV, and, boy, did I think it was awesome. But ultimately I said "no" to both schools and enrolled at the University of Cincinnati instead. On the way home, I was very quiet and I remember my parents were just astonished at what I'd done. Shoot, I did not even know what I was doing, but I felt as if I made the right decision, not playing football and just going and enjoying college for what it was worth. Both parents totally supported me in my decision and they were happy that I choose UC, because they both went to school there. That is where they had met each other.

I was eighteen years old, getting ready to graduate high school and go off to college in three months. Our house was thirty minutes from campus, so I would commute every day to school and still would continue to work at Convenient Food Mart all the way through college. Working there began to be a way of life for me. I would show up for work an hour early, and stay two hours late. Looking back on this, I realize that I was using work as a way to stay away from home. My parents were still in the fighting mode about Dad, his drinking, and his jobs. Money was tight, but his drinking was the biggest issue. He used to say, "I do not have a problem." But even at nineteen years old, and despite the fact that I'd never even heard of A.A., it was clear to me that the problem was beginning to accelerate at a faster speed than I had ever seen it before.

My dad had a job in sales, and I remember coming home one day and finding a "For Sale" sign in our front yard. I came in and began to cry. I was sitting on the hearth of the fireplace, just going into a rage and yelling and screaming at my dad. It was not a fun day in the Serger household. As I see it now, I was getting a gut check to adulthood. The house was up for sale due to finances. Dad was just not mustering up, and money was tight. Mom could not afford to save both the house and the family with her job, so she chose to save the family. The house was on the market for all of two days, and the next day after I'd vented my rage, the house was taken off the market for good. I do not know what my parents did to hold onto it and our family, but it was as if I had done it, by putting a lot of pressure on them to make the relationship work.

I know it was not me that took them to the next level, nor was it my brother, but sending two kids to private schools when your primary bread winner was bringing in very little income must have been tough. I am sure that pressure cooker just finally exploded in their faces. Looking back, I often wondered why they did not pull us out and send us to public schools. I realize now that they simply wanted what was best for their two sons, Saint Xavier and McNicholas High School; two schools that were very good for my brother and me but were very bad for my parents' finances. My dad was a dreamer when it came to himself, but allowing my brother and me to graduate from two good schools was just like him; putting his sons first.

It was my mom's birthday and I came home from work with two boxes of cake mix. I was going to make her a birthday cake. At nineteen years old, I had never made a cake on my own, but I made the cake. It was a double-decker and, boy, did it look good. Mom came home from work, my brother was there and my dad got home from work. We sat down and had a great dinner, and then I presented her with the cake. But as soon as she cut the cake, water came pouring out of it, just gushing out. I had no idea what went wrong until I came to find out that I'd doubled up all the ingredients to the cake. I felt so bad, but Mom thought it was the best birthday present that she had ever received and gave me a hug and kiss. Then it all started downhill from there.

Dad had been drinking that day, and said that he would eat the cake. He took a bite and could not eat any more. Then Mom and he got into an argument over why Jimmy had to make the cake. Why didn't Dad buy a cake? I knew it was not going to be good, so I drove down to Convenient Food Mart and hung out there with Brian, the owner, for a while until things calmed down. My brother ended up coming down as well. Looking back, Convenient Food Mart was the place to go and get comfort away from home.

My dad's condition just seemed to get worse and worse. At the same time, the demand for my dad as a salesman became less and less. The loss of his ability to get work was, I feel, what put him into the gradual tailspin. Added to this, my brother and I both graduated high school. The events, the social world of the booster clubs and the school board meetings disappeared; he was no longer a part of the scene and I think he was feeling no longer needed. Being involved in as many activities as he was over those six years, it had to have been a big blow to him. I think it was the fact that family was becoming second for the first time in his life, and he could not control his state of mind. To watch your dad hit this road is nothing that I would wish on any family, no matter what the circumstances. My dad was about to hit what I thought was rock bottom.

It was January 30, 1990 (again, my mom's birthday) and I was closing down Convenient Food Mart. My shift was until midnight, after which I would go to the bank and drop off the deposit, and then I would drive home. When I arrived home it was 12:30. As I walked up the stairs, my mom called my name. I came in, and she asked me if I had seen or heard from Dad. Of course, I said "No." She said that he did not come home and that it was not like him to stay out this late. Not twenty minutes later, the phone rang. It was the Hamilton County Police Department who were calling to inform us that Dad had been in an accident. He was driving under the influence and they had him down at the station. Mom and I got into the car, and in five minutes we arrived at the station. There he stood, behind bars, with a bloody lip and a few cuts, but nothing too bad. My mom was able to go in and talk to him, but she came out and said to the policeman that he seemed to be getting worse by the minute while she was talking to him. They went in with her and realized he was not drunk, but jacked up on pills. He confessed that he had tried to kill himself with a huge dose of pills and orange juice.

They rushed him to Mercy Hospital where he was admitted right into the ER. They evaluated him and determined that his stomach needed to be pumped. My mom and I were in the room with him. Seeing your dad in jail is bad, but being in the room with him and hearing the doctors pump his stomach was a whole other experience. Here was my dad, right in front of me, having the worst day of his life, and I was there to witness the whole thing first hand. To see your dad lying there helpless and confused is something that happens to other families, I thought to myself; this could never happen to us. We are a strong family, we love each other very much, and we are there for each other all the time. Yet, today was my mom's birthday, and here is my dad; car accident, suicidal, and getting his stomach pumped all in one night. Once again, it was my dad who had to come first; out of all of the days in the year, he had to pick this day to think of himself. This one night would change my relationship with my family for six years.

It turned out that Dad had lost another job. Again, he'd been acting like he was going to work, when in reality he was just going off and doing what he did best at the time – drink. He would rather lie to his wife and his family than come clean with the fact that he had been let go because of poor sales, a result of his drinking. He did not want to lie anymore, he did not want to hurt the family anymore – so he thought we would be better off without him. He grabbed a bunch of pills and drank them down, lay down in the back of the car, and blacked out. Waking up, he'd decided to drive home, but he drove through a construction zone, hitting construction cones, and the police were called.

Dad was treated for all his problems, and was released back to our family about a week later. Dad had to go to A.A. meetings, and he and Mom went to marriage counseling. I just stayed focused on lifting weights and trying to graduate from college. I was going for an Associate's degree and I would graduate from school in December of 1991. Over the next six months as I worked toward graduation, things came in and out of focus for me. My dad's and my relationship was still strong, and yet at the same time it was weak. My mom and I became very close, and our relationship was stronger than it had ever been.

That year, the Gulf War was going on and I remember driving over the suspension bridge that connects downtown Cincinnati to Kentucky with my friend John Messiter. I told him I was going to sign up for the war. I was joking, but there was a lot of confusion going through my head, and I was always intrigued with the military. In October of 1991, I went to a Navy recruiter and got the ball rolling. I was to graduate in December, and then I would go into the Navy in April of 1992.

My final quarter of school was a very good one and a very bad one. I was beginning to drink a little too much; I was in a fraternity, and I lived in the frat house. It was so bad that even my friends began to take notice, and told me I was drinking too much. I was mad at the world, but I was unable to confess to them or to anyone that I was hurting inside. I missed my dad very much, but I too had to find myself. I moved back home for four months and continued work at Convenient Food Mart.

My dad was back in the house and still living his life the best that he could. He had a job and was sober for over eight months. A.A. is set up as a day-to-day operation; once an alcoholic, always an alcoholic. Dad began to slip a little here and there, but he would say, "I have it under control." I started to work out three times a day, so that I could be ready for the Navy. My dad's school buddy owned a huge family fitness center. Dad called him up and explained that I needed a three-month pass. They did not sell three-month passes, but with my dad knowing so many people, this gentleman was willing to break the rules just once for me, since I was going off to the Navy and not just taking advantage of the three-month pass.

But that was the relationship I had with my dad. He would always go to bat for me, no matter what. I never really understood the contradictions in my dad's behavior, and still don't, to this day. How could a man who had everything in life, a great wife, two great kids, great house, and great friends, just quit on them like that, for a beer or mixed drink? *Denial* — and no, that is not a river in Egypt. I came across that line in the book *Understanding the 12 Steps* by Terrance T. Gorski, and I believe it to be so true. My dad was in *denial*. It is a state of mind that controlled him in every aspect of his life. Why didn't he just come clean and admit that he had a problem? Why did he have to hurt Mom so much? Why did he have to hurt my brother and me? The reason is *denial*. No other explanation whatsoever is needed. Once someone admits to the problem, they are on the way to greatness. But that greatness would have to come another day, for I left for the Navy and he was still sipping a few beers.

4TH INNING

"MOST PEOPLE WHO SUCCEED
IN THE FACE OF SEEMINGLY IMPOSSIBLE
CONDITIONS ARE PEOPLE WHO SIMPLY
DON'T KNOW HOW TO QUIT."
– Robert Schuller

HE WILL NOT BE THERE

I joined the Navy in 1992, and was sent to Great Lakes Training Facility in Chicago. After eight weeks of training came graduation day, and my dad, Mom, my brother, and Grandpa and Grandma came to see me graduate. After I graduated, I was sent to Virginia for eight weeks of school, and then shipped off to Yokosuka, Japan. There, I would live on board the *USS Independence* for four years. I was not able to come home for two years, and when the chance came I bought the ticket and came home to Cincinnati. It was as it had been the day I left. I came home to find out the "same old, same old" was still happening with my family, but what was heartbreaking was the fact that I had to go back to Japan to conclude my four years. When I got back to Japan, I decided that I would return to Cincinnati one more time over Christmas to see them, and then I wouldn't go home for another year and a half when I got out. When I came home it was the same again, because Dad was still drinking. I remember one time in 1994 Mom told me that she had confronted him nicely on his drinking. He had insisted that he had it under control. I trusted her and him, but *denial* was even starting to set in with my mom, and I could tell that she was struggling to cope with that.

When I was in Japan, I would receive letters from family and friends. But the one that has remained etched in my mind was the letter I received from my dad about his and Mom's marriage. It was a nice letter, but he told me bluntly that he and she were probably going to be getting a divorce. I had never, ever in my days as a young man imagined that my parents would ever file for divorce. That only happened to other families, not the Serger family. I too was kind of in denial, as I see it, since I was egotistical. I would much rather have had my parents engaged in battles and quarrels indefinitely, than to file for divorce. But living away from home makes it a lot easier to deal with issues, as opposed to being there, live and in person. My brother was the one who I really felt the worst for. I was his big brother and I was halfway around the world on my own expedition. He and I would make up for lost time when I got out of the Navy.

It was Christmas Day, 1995, just four months before I would get out of the Navy, and I decided to go to Christmas Mass on the base. I walked in, and the church was absolutely beautiful. I had never been there before in the three years I'd lived there, but this time it was going to be different. I walked in and sat down.

There must have been four hundred people in that church and everyone was with their families except me. Low and behold, the singing started, and I was feeling very good about myself. Then it came time for the sign of peace, and that is when it dawned on me that I missed my family. I left three quarters of the way through it, for I was crying and out of my element – so I went to the gym instead. I loved being in the Navy. I saw thirteen countries and back-packed all through Asia myself – but I was born to be surrounded by my family. The next day, I went to see a movie on base and it too was about Christmas, and a dysfunctional family. I left the theater and went straight to the phone center to call my parents.

My mom answered the phone, and I began to cry on the phone, and then she began to cry. I loved hearing her voice, and it softened me up knowing that in a few months I would be home. That one phone call put my life into perspective. I loved the Navy, and I really considered re-joining, but I knew that I had a magnificent family back home waiting for me. The Navy gave me everything and then some, which I expected from the Navy. It gave me structure, discipline, leadership, character, and a work ethic that would shape my life. I often wonder what would have happened to my dad, if he had gone to Vietnam. Would he have grown into a man? Would he have had structure in his life? Would he have gained time management skills? I know for a fact he would have understood the value of teamwork and unity, instead of putting himself first.

So in 1996, I left the Navy and headed back to Cincinnati. When I arrived home, it was just good to be there. I was home fourteen days when I landed the job that I still have to this day, working for Home City Ice. When I got used to being at home, I understood that my parents were still trying to work things out, as they had always tried to do. Getting a divorce was always being talked about, but it never really happened. Dad was still drinking a little here and there, but nothing as far as I could tell was out of control. What was out of control was the idea of me living at home with them. My brother and I moved out and got a condo in Northern Kentucky, close to his job and close to mine. In the one year we lived there, not once did my dad ever come over to see it. It was as if he was not going to go out of his way to see where we lived. I do not know if he was afraid to see us, or whether he was just too busy to come over. That bothered me somewhat. Here we were, the closest of friends, and not once did he come over and just say "hi." He never even took us out for lunch. Shoot, he never took us out to have a beer, which is a good thing.

I had re-enrolled back at the University of Cincinnati to continue my schooling, and that year the Bearcat basketball team was ranked #1 in the country, under the guidance of Bob Huggins. I had season tickets as a student and who do you think I took to see five games? – my dad and my brother. It was so funny; here we were, twenty-five years old, twenty-three years old and fifty years old, all sitting in the student section. We had a momentous time at every game. I would buy us dinner or my brother would buy, and sometimes my dad would buy. Sitting in the section, beer was served and my dad would have a couple, and so would my brother and I. The point is that all three of us were enjoying what we had always enjoyed. But that was my dad at this stage of his life. I had to go out of my way to invite him to functions, because he wouldn't be bothered to invite me. *Selfish*.

When I started at Home City Ice in 1996, the first person I saw was the secretary, Tarla, and from that day on I worked on building up the nerve to ask her out. There was something about her that appealed to me. She had gone to Anderson High School, which was the public high school down the street from mine. She graduated one year later than I did, in 1990, and she lived in Anderson Township. She was and still is a very exuberant, loving, kind person, the person I looked forward to talking to at the end of each day of work. I would sit in her office for hours, just chatting and laughing with her about all the people she and I knew. I saw in her a person that was loving and considerate, and I was passionately head over heels for her. I always wanted to ask her out on a date, but I was so nervous. It was at my first Christmas party that I finally asked her if she would drive down to the event with me, and she said yes. I had moved back home in 1997 to save money, and she lived in an apartment just three miles down the road, so we went together. We went to a few other functions together as well, but it was not until 1998 that I would begin to date Tarla seriously. The woman was a complete knockout, and still is to this day. She and I would have some grand days ahead of us, and some rough waters in the way as well. I love this woman with everything I have; she is what I would describe as the ultimate companion on the face of the earth. Yes, we have issues to deal with. But when we were just starting to date, Tarla and I would face our greatest challenge together, much sooner in our relationship than most couples have to deal with.

At the same time my life was changing for the better, my dad's life was getting ready to take a nosedive. He'd lost his job for whatever reason, and so he'd decided to venture into real estate. Shoot, his networking alone would take him into the 25th century, no problem. But that was yet to be seen; talk is one thing, but doing is another. It was spring of 1999, I had asked Tarla to marry me, and of course she'd said yes. I was so happy to be with her that sometimes I would even drop a note on her car after work, just to say I loved her. The wedding day was set for March 25, 2000. The new millennium; what a date it would be. But getting there was going to be a challenge. Mom finally had enough of Dad's issues, and out the door he went. It was not due to poor communication on my mom's side, it was the fact that Dad was not listening to what she had to say. In the months leading up to this, Dad had been sleeping on the couch; Dad had also been lying to her about finances, just to protect her from the truth. Once again, that same old broken record – only this time, my mom took a stand, and they separated. Two weeks later, the same week as their wedding anniversary, they got a divorce.

That year, Dad landed a cute little neighborhood of new construction right around the corner from Tarla's apartment. Fourteen houses were to be built and sold for $99,000 to $114,000. Dad, now "Mr. Real-Estate," was in charge of the subdivision. He did his networking and landed his second customers, Tarla and me. We were to get married in March of 2000, and the house was to be done in December of 1999. Dad did all the legwork with us, and was always willing to lend a hand to help guide us on our new acquisition. It was a very cute bi-level with hardwood floors and a little back yard. The coolest thing about it to me was the fact it was a brand new house. How many newly married couples can get a new house? Not many, but then again, we were thirty years old. In the summer of 1999, Dad moved into an apartment right down the street from where we were to live. I would stop over every once in a while but that was it. Busy with marriage plans and work, I did not have time or even make time to be with him. Mom would invite us over and we would accept, for she was the one about whom I was more worried. They had been married for thirty years, and now for the first time she was coming home to an empty house. With my brother getting married the year before, and me the following year, she had enough to keep her busy. She was and still is an interior decorator, and a darn good one at that. She had plenty of work to keep her busy. I guess after being married for so long to a great friend, things began to collapse around her as well, in small bites. She always said that she was fine and happy with the decision she'd made, but in reality it was much harder for her than we all realized. Being married for that long, making the decision that she'd made – who wouldn't be hurting?

Then came the day that would change our lives forever as a family, the day Dad decided that he would go off and do something really foolish. You see, with all that was transpiring in my life for the better, Dad's life that was changing for the worse. Two months before we were to close on our house, credit companies began calling, looking for Dad. He had purchased a couch, a chair and other furniture, and he was unable to pay them back. Mom was getting all the phone calls about his credit. At the real estate agency where he worked, the police showed up to take my dad in for questioning on his credit problems. My wife Tarla knew all about my Dad's issues, but what would take place next was beyond anything conceivable. I'd never imagined that my Dad, my Superman, would come off as a freeloader, much less a criminal, but that is what happened.

It was fall of 1999, and Mom had called the house to explain that she had been getting odd phone calls from random gas stations, looking for my dad. They were looking for him to pay them back for his cigars and gas. She asked us to come over and to spend the night, because the phone calls were starting to pour in at all hours the last day or so, so we complied and went over to comfort her. Tarla and I were worried, but my mom was worried as well. Having thrown him out of the house was one thing, but to not love him anymore was another. Their affection for each other was untouchable. They'd always had a very close relationship, had both believed that they were the perfect couple.

The minute we arrived at the house, I could tell that Mom was getting very apprehensive about Dad. She would laugh a little, or joke about what was going on, but it was obvious to me that under her joking, she was worried sick. She made us dinner, and we just stayed up and talked. Another phone call came in from a gas station in Batesville, Indiana. Dad had gone there, gotten gas and cigars, went to pay for them, and then had said that he'd forgotten his wallet. He'd given the gas station attendant his real estate card and told him that he would be back to pay for it. Needless to say, he did not come back;

he just drove away, ever further and further away from Cincinnati, but to where? No one knew.

Another day passed and still no answers as to where he was. Then, finally, after two days on the run, he called home. He had been arrested in Indianapolis for skipping out on a food bill. But what had really happened was that his license plate had been listed on the police system, he was illegally parked, and they caught him. He was taken to Marion County Jail in Indianapolis. There was a whole list of misdemeanors waiting for him to pay back. When we told his brother Ken that Dad was in jail, Ken, my brother and I drove to Indianapolis to see Dad. I remember us all talking on the way there about what had transpired. We all came to the agreement that alcohol had taken over Dad's life 100%. It was no longer an issue that we all could sweep under the rug. This was and is the reason that my dad was no longer seen as a buddy by me. I'd loved him with everything I had and he'd loved me just as much, but Dad was two people living one life. He chose the easy path, and that was alcohol.

It took us a little under three hours to get there, and upon arriving I remember looking around at all the other people going into jail. Not one person looked like anyone I would hang out with. They looked as if they should have been in jail. I know that sounds harsh, but seeing what goes on in jail, and all the circumstances that take people there – that just did not fit my notion of our family. A coach, a school board president – that guy was in jail, my dad, *Superman*? This does not happen to good people – but then again, was my dad a good person? I would have liked to think so, but for the moment he was not. Going through check-in, I was a nervous wreck. Never had I gone through metal detectors or a pat-down like that before.

On the ride, I had thought that we all were going to get the chance to see him, but unfortunately only two us were allowed to go back. I decided it was best for my uncle Ken and my brother to go. I knew my dad and I were close, so letting him see his brother and his other son was more important. I do not regret doing that, even though Ken offered to let me go. Letting Dad's brother see him was important, and it turned out fine. As we drove home they both described Dad as not being himself; he was a stranger, someone who looked like death, someone we'd only see on *America's Most Wanted*.

What led up to the whole outcome was the fact that Dad was living on his own, with no one around to watch and see firsthand what he was doing. There was no one there to say NO, no one there to ask where he'd been. Dad was a bachelor for the first time in a long time, and a terrible bachelor he was. When he and Mom got the divorce, Dad was given a cash amount, but that cash ran out faster than he had ever foreseen, between rent, food, bills – and most important, alcohol. He said he hated himself for a failed marriage, failed career, failed everything. Dad was a child for the first time without a parent to take care of him, which had been my mom's role. The way I see it, Dad could not handle anything on his own; someone had to be there to comfort him, shelter him and protect him. He'd learned how to get another person to show him the way, without his having to take ownership of his own actions and own consequences. But drinking every night is what he did to relieve the stress, he said. He ran out of money, and he had no other choice but to run away from his fears. The greatest fear of all was telling someone that he needed help.

A week went by and he was extradited to Cincinnati, to Hamilton County Jail. In the meantime Tarla and I were about to close on our house, and of course, Dad was unable to be our real-estate agent, so his boss filled in for him. Dad no longer had the job. It was awesome to move into a new, freshly built house. Tarla had worked very hard her whole life, and finally she and I were able to have something of our own for the first time. We put a fence in around back, and got a dog. We even were able to get a new car; things in our life were going great leading up to our wedding day, now just six months away. We were very, very happy. Things just seemed to click with her and me, we had hopes that my dad's life would get back on track, and Mom now seemed at ease, knowing that Dad was all right. She was very lonely; she would stop over at our house on occasion just to see how we were doing. She seemed to be getting used to living the life of a single mom, but I believe deep down inside, it was just a front. She is and always will be a strong-willed person. She could do anything she wanted. Life had a strange twist on it, but she was able to make adjustments to keep on the path and not stray off it.

Dad was faced with misdemeanor charges and was forced to pay back everything that he could. He was then put back into society, nothing else. Five thousand dollars was waiting at our house from his boss. He received the commission for selling and listing our house, and a few others that had sold while he was gone. Christmas had come and gone, and now it was down to the wire for Tarla and me to make preparations for the wedding, just four months away. We were getting very excited about the day, and had the catering company all lined up and the flowers ordered. We would be married at her dad's church.

In the meantime, Dad had nowhere to stay when he was discharged from jail. His brother picked him up, and was gracious enough to line up a short-term rental deal with the inn just down the road from everyone, by the interstate. Five thousand dollars in his hands was pretty good money to start off with. I would go and see him a few times after he got out, making sure he was okay, but I had a wedding to get ready for. He would tell me that he had a job lined up at Home Depot, then he would say that the interview was tomorrow, then it led to "I am interviewing with Lowes." Then it was "I am interviewing with so and so…" and on and on and on. We all started to notice that Dad was still unable to come clean with anyone in regards to telling the truth. It was killing everyone. My brother and I took him out for lunch and he said, "Oh yeah, job hunting is going great. Few apps here, a few apps there." But, somehow it never wound up with him getting a job. Having been out of jail for only a month, he was already up to his old tricks and lying. To this day, I believe that he was not drinking at that point; then again, I could not be around him 24/7.

The biggest day of my life was now just two weeks away and my mom had not seen my dad in six months. The wedding day was going to be magnificent – family and friends would be there, but I had to make a decision on whether or not to invite my dad. It was the toughest call I had ever had to make. I remember that it was a Friday when I called my dad's best friend Paul, and asked if he could meet me on Saturday for lunch. While we ate and had a beer, I just flat-out asked him what I should do – for he knew that was the reason for the meeting. He leaned over and said, "Jimmy, whatever decision you make will be the right decision." Paul and Dad had been best friends since they were five years old and this man just said to me that whatever decision I made about Dad, he would support me.

I was torn for weeks on what to do, but not inviting Dad was the right decision to make. I never quit on my dad, not once. I had to this time, for good reason. The reason was so that he would finally understand that his getting rehab, him getting healthy, him focusing on him, was the way to recovery. I'd never thought about it in those terms exactly, but for some reason a Higher Power was looking out for my family that year. I am not a very religious person at all, but that year, in 2000, a miracle did happen. I got married to the most wonderful person in the world, and my dad was not there to see it. He was left out so that he could understand that it was about family, and not about him and his problems. Two encouraging moments in one year – wow – powerful stuff, if you ask me.

Not having my dad at my wedding was not fun; I sure missed him being there. I would have loved to have him attend, but I made the best decision, through guidance of my family, his friend Paul, my mom and, most importantly, the guidance of my wife. There is a picture in our wedding album of my wife and I and my mom; no Dad. I look at that picture and regret that he was not there. But I did it for the right reasons – I did it for him, my dad, my friend, my buddy, the person that I love.

As I sat in front of everyone looking at the attendees, I realized that from that moment in time things were on the up and up for my family. Dad was not at the wedding, but everyone there understood why he was not present. His addiction, his relapse, his demons were at his doorstep to face him head on. My dad had a choice to make, either to accept responsibility for his actions and the consequences of his decisions, or he was to eventually just die; very straightforward and to the point. No one ever quit on my dad at all; we gave him every opportunity in this world to help guide him on the path to sobriety.

Now more than ever, Dad was beginning to come full circle in his awareness of his problem. At least, that was the impression he gave us. Physically, we had to quit on my dad, and I mean everyone had to quit on him; his dad, his wife, his friends, and all of his family. We had no other choice. We all still talked to him and checked up on him, but we had to let Dad do it on his own. He had to come clean with this problem; we could not do it for him. We would all have loved to have him at my wedding. Everyone understood that we must let go of Dad physically, but not mentally. Quitting on someone you love is the worst thing that anyone can do to another, but we were all with him spiritually. Not once at the wedding did anyone bring his name up to me, not once did someone say *it sure would have been nice to have seen your dad*. Yet, weeks before and weeks after the wedding, people would ask me how he was doing. You see, what my dad did not realize was the fact that people loved him for who he was, not for the man he thought he should be.

Just a month after the best day of my life, the world came crashing down on the family. It was Mother's Day, and my uncle Ken had just gotten a phone call from my dad, on a borrowed quarter – to tell him and, I am sure, others, that he was *powerless*. My dad, slurring his speech, told Ken that he was at Coney Island's Amusement Park's parking lot, down by the Ohio River. He sounded exhausted and totally delusional. This, we all knew, was not a good thing. I went to work for two days knowing my dad was at the inn, looking for a job; then I came to find out the bridge that I drove across every day to work, he had been living under; hiding, I guess, unable to face the world. He tried to take his own life again, tried to jump off of that bridge.

It turned out that while Dad was at the inn, he never came out except to go to McDonalds across the parking lot to grab a bite to eat. He had lied to everyone about his job situation, a fact to which we'd all caught on. Mom and he had no contact at all during this time, which was great for him, and bad for him. His brother Ken and I, as well as my brother, would check up on him; Ken would even take him to church on Sundays. My Dad was totally depressed, as he recalls. But no one could watch him 24/7, no one could babysit him, we all had our own lives to worry about and focus on. After 60 days or so at the inn, all of his money ran out, and the truth came out too about his job hunting. Dad says he felt so worthless, and was so depressed that he just could not face another day. So he walked down to the Ohio River and slept for two nights under the bridge, thinking that his time was up and he had to do something about it. He was planning to take his own life.

In those 60 days, my dad claims that he did not drink, and I would have to say that I believe him. Looking back at our past as a family, the one thing that had been missing in my dad's life that he now was gaining back was God. We were Catholic, and for years I was an altar boy, as was my brother in grade school. We went to church all the time as a family, but the older we got, and the more Dad was drinking, the quicker that word "church" faded out of our family. Yes, we went on Christmas, Easter and other big holidays – but we did not go all the time like we had, during my eight years of grade school. The way I see it is that Ken and his wife did something truly wonderful for my dad by taking him to church. If he did not drink in those 60 days, and he called his brother to cry out for help, it was because Dad for the first time in many, many years had called out to God and God had heard his call. Dad was not just calling his brother; Dad was calling on all of the family. For the first time, Dad was saying, "I need help" – and that cry for help was about to be answered.

I am correct in saying that things just kept on going further and further south for him the last three years. He never could get a grip on his drinking, and the rest of us had no other choice but to seek the deepest parts of our souls to help him. You see, after Ken picked up Dad at the parking lot, Ken, Grandpa, and I decided that enough was enough, and that we had to finally allow my dad to hit rock bottom. We paid $250 dollars each to post his probation money so he would not be arrested and sent off to jail again. All $5,000 was gone, and he was living out another lie to protect himself, to try and live up to expectations that didn't exist outside of his own mind. He just could not see the vision of himself getting sober; he just could not see that it is okay to be ill, or okay to be angry. Dad was convinced that he had to lie in order to protect himself – but to protect himself from what? The whole circle of his life was to lie, cover up, get a job, lie, and cover up, get a job. This to him was the road to take as a man, instead of being a real man and admitting that he was confused and helpless. He saw fit to hurt others with his lying and his drinking, and let that circle continue until he could remedy the situation. But in all my years as a young man that never happened for him. He just could not fix his root problem, which was *drinking*.

This time was going to be different; no one in the family was going to allow Dad to stay with them, nor would they help him to cover up all that had transpired with him. Homeless; wow, what a word. My Dad, Jim Serger, Mr. Baseball, had nowhere to go. He was, for the first time in his life, unable to go home and start the circle of his past life over. Once again, the whole world was revolving around my dad and his needs; not the fact his oldest son was married, but the fact he needed help, and he needed it quick.

He was admitted to the University of Cincinnati Hospital. There he underwent two weeks of evaluations and it was determined that Dad would be put on the waiting list for the Prospect House on the west side of Cincinnati. Life at the Prospect House is not easy, and it is not intended to be. It is a program that is intended to help men get their lives back in order, one step at a time, whether their addiction is to drugs or to liquor. The program is designed to allow men to gradually step forward instead of stepping backwards, and it is a very successful program. But one must be willing to accept it for what it is, and not what he want its to be; A.A. meetings, spiritual groups, and the list goes on and on. In the meantime, while waiting for the Prospect House, he was admitted to the halfway house, Mount Airy Shelter. This program works exclusively with homeless men to provide emergency shelter and services that help clients solve many of the problems that have left them with no place to call home. This is the transition from prison, or off the streets with an addiction. It is a home that is set up like an old World War II barracks, on the west side of Cincinnati. There, men can begin to come off the streets, or they can stay on the streets. It is run like a military unit and there are very strict rules; come in drunk, you're thrown into the streets. Come in on drugs, you are thrown into the streets. Priests and other spiritual figures come over all the time to give encouragement, and most of all to lend an ear for everyone to open up their thoughts. The halfway house was the path less taken by many addicts, but family support and a ton of love is what got Dad to the halfway house, and that includes my mom's help. His attitude, his mental awareness began to take a healthier shape and, having hit his ultimate low, he was about to take one little step higher each day as he confronted his dilemma.

The following poem is the best way to explain my feelings and thinking about my dad over the 10 years from 1990-2000. Those years were the years that I believe I missed my dad the most. Feelings, thoughts, regrets, abandonment, love, happiness, caring, fatherhood, manhood; these words described our relationship leading up to my wedding day, and for a little while after it. Watching your dad who at one time was the team leader, the platoon sergeant, get hurt, be in jail, fall off the wagon and follow the path of denial, was truly devastating to me. All I ever wanted was for my dad to be a dad. I never wanted him to be anything else.

WHO WILL CRY FOR THE LITTLE BOY?

By Antwone Fisher

Who will cry for the little boy?
Lost and all alone.
Who will cry for the little boy?
Abandoned without his own?
Who will cry for the little boy?
He cried himself to sleep.
Who will cry for the little boy?
He never had for keeps.
Who will cry for the little boy?
He walked the burning sand.
Who will cry for the little boy?
The boy inside the man.
Who will cry for the little boy?
Who knows well hurt and pain.
Who will cry for the little boy?
He died again and again.
Who will cry for the little boy?
A good boy he tried to be.
Who will cry for the little boy?
Who cries inside of me?

By Antwone Fisher from *Who Will Cry for the Little Boy?*

Antwone Q. Fisher, *Who Will Cry for the Little Boy?*, http://antwonefisher.net

God works in mysterious ways. We have all heard the saying from time to time. Does God work in truly mysterious ways? Or does God allow human beings to love and care for other human beings' welfare, having not known the person whom they are carrying for? That to me is how God worked for my dad. He gave my dad a choice and Dad took the path less traveled by. Robert Frost wrote the following poem ninety years ago. This describes my dad's journey to sobriety. This is the path that he had to choose in order for him to confront his demons and return to a life of family, friends, and most importantly, a life full of meaning.

THE ROAD NOT TAKEN (1915)
Robert Frost

TWO roads diverged in a yellow wood,
And sorry I could not travel both
And be one traveler, long I stood
And looked down one as far as I could
To where it bent in the undergrowth;

Then took the other, as just as fair,
And having perhaps the better claim,
Because it was grassy and wanted wear;
Though as for that the passing there
Had worn them really about the same,

And both that morning equally lay
In leaves no step had trodden black.
Oh, I kept the first for another day!
Yet knowing how way leads on to way,
I doubted if I should ever come back.

I shall be telling this with a sigh
Somewhere ages and ages hence:
Two roads diverged in a wood, and I –
I took the one less traveled by,
And that has made all the difference.

Robert Frost, *Mountain Interval* (New York: Henry Holt, 1921), pp. 9. PS 3511 R94 M6 ROBA.

The similarities in each poem share a common point, in that Dad and I were feeling very saddened over the years and were both crying out for help. Each of us took different paths to fight off the crying; I chose the Navy, and he chose alcohol. Each of us had a little boy inside, crying out for attention and love. Each of us was deeply hurting, and each of us could see that through each other's actions. Not having my dad at my wedding was a path I had to choose, but with the help of friends I chose the correct path. Dad listened to new friends and had to choose the path of sobriety. Both were hard to follow. The true north was the position that we both were searching for, in getting his life back in order. Love is that true north; quitting on him was not option B, it was option A. Staying on course and laying out a course to get there was our way of releasing the little boy, and confronting our demons as men. God gave both of us guidance, awareness, stability, and a choice to make his sobriety come true. God only meets us halfway, as I see it. He sets us up with new mentors, new programs, new venues we never thought existed. But with those gifts comes the gift of giving back. 50% + 50% = 100%. God gave us 50% and it was up to Dad, me, my wife, Mom, Grandpa, his brothers, my brother, his friend Paul and cousin, Donny to give the other 50% to get our family back to 100%.

Tarla and I would go over a few times a month to see Dad at the halfway house. Sometimes it would just be me. It would take a half hour to drive over and see him, but it was worth the drive. When I first went up there, I was expecting something like the kind of rehab center that I had seen on TV; big, new, acres of green grass, water fountains, very elaborate. But as I drove up, I saw that all it was, was an old World War II barracks. Nothing extravagant, but it was a place to lay his head and a place that would turn his life around. Dad and I would talk for a few hours, and I would drop off cigars for him. He would tell a few stories about how rough it was in there with the other guys, in that most of them were living on and off of the streets, halfway in society and halfway out. I never understood that, until Dad was a part of the program. He would tell a story about a man who came back drunk and was not allowed to enter the halfway house, because they threw him out. He was allowed to go downtown and stay at one of the mission shelters, but the halfway house would not allow people in who were drunk or who had been drinking. It was set in stone that you were not going to jeopardize their mission in life and that mission was to treat one person at a time, no matter the cost. It might sound very harsh, but it was to the point, like a fraternity, or the military. No one person's need is greater than the group's needs are.

That is where Dad's mission in life began to take hold. His mission, if he chose to accept it, was to get himself sober, one day at a time; that was it. The program was all about him and for once that was a good thing. He had to be selfish; he needed just to think of himself, for if the path he chose was to lead him where he wanted to go, he had to take time for his needs and that was to be clean and sober. Bill Wilson created the 12 Steps to sobriety program years ago to help individuals confront their problems through a step-by step-process. The program is a path, like the poem says, that one must be willing to accept in order to get healed of the disease. It's true; once an alcoholic, always an alcoholic. However, when facing a calamity as my dad did, facing the 12 Steps head-on would enable him to address his needs and move on to other avenues that would impact his life and help him to stay sober.

Seeing Dad transformed every day from June 2000 to January 2001 was astounding for everyone. Although the program was working for him, he was still on the waiting list for the Prospect

House, and soon his number would come up. Mom, not having seen my dad in almost nine months, had heard how wonderfully he was doing with the program, and she decided to go and check on him firsthand. She was intrigued with the idea of seeing his progress transforming him into something that she had been hoping for, for a long time. Since he hadn't seen her for a while, I would venture to say that Dad was a little nervous. He and Mom had to confront each other eventually, either during Dad's rehab or after he finished. This, as I see it, never really has an end.

Love; that is the key component to this family. Love is what got my dad to the halfway house; love is what got my mom to see my dad. Love is what drove my brother to see him, my dad's brother, my grandpa, and my other uncles, his cousin Donny, and his friend Paul. All of these people were the driving force behind my dad's success in staying sober. With Dad being sober, he finally came to grips with the fact that people love him for who he is and not for what he was. The titles he had over the years were just that – titles. You do not need a brand name to be a leader. All these years, living up to these expectations was driving Dad into the ground. *Love is in the Air*, that was a popular song in the '70s, but today in the 21st century, that song is still alive and breathing in our family. The halfway house was just that, halfway. By no means was Dad able to go back to society, having finished the program. Dad's journey, as well as mine, was to take another step forward. The Prospect House had just allowed him to enter their program.

5TH INNING

"A TRULY RICH MAN IS ONE WHOSE
CHILDREN RUN TO HIS ARMS WHEN HIS
HANDS ARE EMPTY."
– Author unknown

I WILL COME VISIT YOU

**GOD GRANT ME THE SERENITY TO ACCEPT
THE THINGS I CANNOT CHANGE,
THE COURAGE TO CHANGE THE THINGS I CAN,
AND THE WISDOM TO KNOW THE DIFFERENCE.**

This prayer has been with my family for a long time. It was on my dad's nightstand in 1990, and it has been talked about and spoken in our family many times. The prayer was written by Reinhold Niebuhr as early as 1934. It was to be a part of his sermon for the day. Bill Wilson, co-founder of A.A., heard that prayer and in 1941, he introduced that prayer to A.A. He had it printed up and handed out to the members.

After being at the halfway house for seven months, Dad's mental awareness was starting to come back to life. You see, Dad had to weigh his options for life. Was it going to be liquor, or was it going to be getting sober? The path is a very difficult one to choose, and the halfway house was a steppingstone for what was to come next. With Dad's readiness to concentrate on himself and not on anyone else, he was able to adjust his life around for the first time. Dad's denial was now right in front of him. Let me tell you, it was about time. For years, everyone around him had told him to lay off the booze, to give it up, but Dad could not. It was costing him his family and his friends, and he was unable to see that. The man in him was unwilling to sacrifice that habit at all costs, and it cost him enormously since no one was around to rescue him. Yes, he still had me, my brother, his wife, and the list goes on and on. But we had to let go of him physically in order to get him back mentally. It is very hard for me to explain the reason that I had to turn my back on him, but as I see it, the whole world was not going to turn their backs on him. It did not matter to me if I ever saw him again, because if Dad did not accept that he had a problem, then I was unwilling to accept him into my life again.

I would say that emotionally our relationship was as strong as any other father/son relationship, if not even stronger. He and I would always hug and kiss as if nothing was wrong. I recall one time in high school I threw my arm out pitching a no-hitter against the number one team in the city. He came up to me after the game and gave me a hug and a kiss, for he knew that I had thrown my arm out. He knew too that he had talked to me a few times about the risk for a pitcher in lifting weights, and he knew that weightlifting was what had cost me my arm, but it did not matter to him. He loved me, and I loved him. He supported me, and I supported him. That was our relationship.

The halfway house was that relationship for him and me. He knew that he needed help; we all knew he needed help. This time it was going to work. Why? The incentive was that for the first time in his life, he had nothing to fall back on. Mom and he had gotten a divorce; my brother and I were each married. He was at rock bottom, and he realized what he had done to our family. I would go over and see him, and he was as happy as a clown for the first time in a long time. Why? The reason is, he was climbing a ladder for the first time for his own survival and, boy, was he getting up this ladder fast. He knew that one ladder would lead him to another level, which he had not been to; he would achieve what was necessary at that level, then move up the next ladder to the next level. Each day at the halfway house, Dad's life was becoming more meaningful – not through titles, but through achievements in his personal life. Dad's leadership skills in the house were obvious to everyone that he came across; he was leading others without even knowing that he was. I would drive up and park, and when I would tell the first person I saw that I was looking for Jim, they'd say, "Oh, Jim Serger, I know him; he is in such and such building." You see, his identity knew where to be found, for it was his stellar leadership ability, shining through. The loving, caring person I knew my dad to be, was at that halfway house. "Dad" was the only title that I wanted him to have. Within that word "Dad" is contained leadership, ownership, responsibility, forgiveness, love and the ability to be one's self – and he was doing that, for the first time that I could tell, in a long time.

The survivor in him was achieving more and more every day. Loved ones were coming over to see how he was; his brother, his cousins, his two sons and, of course, his old friend and companion, my mom. You see, for months Mom had hinted around about going over. We said "no" a few times and finally she took it upon herself to go. For the first time they were talking on neutral ground. No other forces were around Dad; no money, no house, no jobs, no car, no bills. He and Mom just talked about Dad getting healthy and, I am sure, the fact that they were meant to be best friends, which in spite of everything, they still were. But Dad had a problem, and Mom was willing to help solve the problem one step more by letting him be aware that she supported him and loved him.

It was January of 2001; Dad finally climbed the last ladder the halfway house had to offer. His seven months or so at the house helped fulfill the social needs, educational needs and medical needs he so desperately wanted to have met. The mission at the halfway house was to get my dad residential help so that he could be discharged into the community. With Dad accomplishing those steps, he was to be accepted into the Prospect House for the next twelve months, or longer if needed. The Prospect House is located in Price Hill, on the west side of Cincinnati and close to the halfway house. The difference is that the Prospect House is a long-term residential program. This program has been around for 40 years and is designed to treat male substance abusers. This passage is straight from their web site, (www.prospect-house.org): *Our joy is to put men back to work, or into college, and back into functioning families, as effective and honest husbands and fathers, men who can work, and men who can love and be loved.*

Just as at the halfway house, I would come over and visit my dad. I was not going to turn my back on him anymore, for I knew that he was giving his all-out best to get himself back on his feet. I know the house gave him all the credentials that he needed to accomplish that goal. The one visit that I remember best was when he received an award for his 200th day of being sober. My wife, my mom and I all drove over to see him there. It was a huge day, and I was not going to miss it for the world. My dad had been at all of my sporting events, all of my practices, and all of my school functions, and I was not going to miss this one. It was a huge deal to be there and sure enough, he was just like himself, introducing all of us to his new friends. Dad loved these guys, all of them from different walks of life, but all having the same thing in common. We had dinner there that night and watched Dad being presented with the award. I was never more proud of my dad than I was that night. I have been proud of him many times; new company car, new fancy job, winning a trip for a sales competition. But for the first time this night, he was awarded for accomplishing something that he'd had to work out on his own. Yes, there was support and encouragement from others, but Dad chose the path not taken in order for him to get this award. As A.A. puts it, *one day at a time.* On the 201st day, it was on to another new day, and on and on it went for him.

In the Prospect House, you had to get a job and start the transformation into the real world, and with that support, Dad was able to land a job with a department store in Western Hills. He was in the men's suits division. This job suited him really well, no pun intended. In college, Dad had sold suits at Pogue's Department Store in downtown Cincinnati and he loved doing it. The new job was great for him; he was able to take control of himself for the first time in over two years. Money was not the most important factor in Dad's getting a job. The importance of that job was that he could begin to align his life back to the True North, as the author Bill George would put it. He had a map all laid out in front of him, and that map had arrows leading from one spot to the next. The true north was how he was going to steer his ship, and he did it to a "T". He missed out on many things, looking back over the past two years, but that to me was of no importance at all, for the future is what we all were focusing on. People say that in order to get a good look at someone's future, look into his past. Well, my friends, the past in Dad's case is a cancelled check. It is over; the past is the past. We all had to focus on the present, and with that, the future was looking so much brighter.

Every day that my dad stayed at the Prospect House was another day of fulfillment. It brought him great pain and happiness at the same time. I remember talking with him, and he was so upset with himself because he wasn't able to attend my wedding. I said to him, "Who cares? The important thing today is that you and I have created something that we have been searching for, and that thing is you being sober." Of course, we hugged and cried.

My dad's job now was to focus his efforts on staying sober, to attend A.A. meetings, and to begin to transform himself back into Jim Serger, the greatest dad of all time. I worked a few days of the week on the west side of town, which allowed me to visit him often at work. I would go over to the department store and visit him sometimes twice a week for while, gradually cutting it back to once a week as his rehab came to an end.

The moment of truth was the fact that my mom was beginning to see how well Dad was doing. She realized for the first time in a long time that he loved her, and that they needed to be together. Love has a strange way of working, and love is what got them back together. I also believe that God got them back together. Yes, they are divorced, but God works in mysterious ways and in this case I believe it was God who was able to allow my mom to quit on my dad, and it was also God that allowed my mom to come over and see him again. God gave her the strength. They were always best friends, and they loved and cared for each other tremendously. It was just the fact that booze got in the way, and Dad did not see it that way. He was sick, and always will be an alcoholic. But coming forth and no longer denying it is what saved their friendship.

UNDERSTANDING THE WORD TEAMWORK

I truly believe that my dad did not grasp that, in order for him to be sober, he needed to understand the value of teamwork. This word **teamwork** is what saved Dad's life. Yes, all 12 Steps of A.A. are what really saved his life, but his truly coming to understand this word is the reason why my dad was able to achieve being sober for over one year. "You can't do it alone" is so true in life; it was not that Larry Bird won all those NBA games; it was the *team* he was on, with a great coach. When the Reds won the World Series in 1990, it took all the players to go the distance. You cannot do anything alone. I do not care what anyone says; even if you write a great paper, someone else created the pencil you are writing with, someone else created the paper you are putting the pencil to. In my dad's life at the Prospect House, it was everyone leading up to the house that helped guide him there, and it was everyone in the Prospect House that guided him up the next ladder, to a new level. As I see it, my dad was *surrounded* by other men who had the same problem, and that was okay, because seeing and believing are two different things. Others deny the fact; others just do not see it. But at the Prospect House you are part of the seeing and the believing. Each person's dreams of staying sober rubbed off on my dad's dreams of staying sober. Through stories and through constant reminders, Dad was able to get a grip on life and see with new clarity how he'd hurt me, and the whole family.

Making amends is where Dad grew a ton in the Prospect House. The blame game was over, and he could see that his denial was the reason why he was sick. Blaming others for your condition is not how you achieve getting sober, nor does it even make you feel good about getting sober. Dad came full circle when he told me that for five hours he sat at a picnic table with a priest and just let all of his thoughts out. He was crying with the priest, and the priest sat there the whole time and listened. It was there that Dad, for the first time, was not fighting the cause, which down the line would be his biggest achievement; staying sober. He was born again, I would say, not as a Bible beater or religious fanatic, but as one who was willing to give in to God. He was letting God transform his life, going from feeling sorry for himself to being a person that would lend an ear to another buddy in the house. Dad's EGO (Edging God Out) was vanishing. Dad's leadership skills were also showing in the house, and making amends with all that he had done was how it had to be. Telling me that he loved me was sure good to hear, but his sobriety was so much better. He was not driven to other paths that he might have taken when he was drinking; this time his head was on straight and his brain was functioning like a human being's.

Dad is a big softy; he has always had a good, kind spirit in him. He is a great friend to me, and I am a great friend to him. That is how I thought the whole time that Dad was living in the Prospect House; he and I fed off each other, and it made our relationship that much stronger. I loved him for who he was, not for what he was. Yes, having a dad who'd played Division One baseball, someone who was selected by the Phillies, someone who was the president of the school board – all of those things were great achievements that made me proud of him, but his sobriety was the greatest achievement he'd ever reached. I have told the baseball stories so many times to my friends that I truly believe that even they were proud of him, but the Prospect House was and is the most difficult accomplishment he had ever made. In spring of 2002, my dad was released from the Prospect House, having met the greatest goal ever laid out in front of him, and that was staying sober for over a year and half.

When Dad was attempting to kill himself in 1990 and again in 1999, I truly believe that his actions were out of love for his family. I feel like Dad just got sick and tired of being sick and tired, as they say in A.A. meetings. That sounds dumb and I know it, but Dad, being as sick as he was, was doing the best that he could, other than coming clean with the fact he had a drinking problem. Killing himself would have been the worst thing that ever happened to our family. Not having my father around seemed like something we'd have to face too soon, and I accepted that as part of our lives, until he came clean with his addiction to alcohol. Dad hitting rock bottom was the epicenter of our lives. It was the one greatest event that I feel changed our lives for the better. He now was living the life of a sober man – a life of meaning, one of love and one that he could call his own and be proud of.

There was a song written by Pearl Jam entitled *Just Breathe*. This song hits me every single time I hear it on the radio, because I believe that it tells the whole story of my dad's and my relationship, not only about the emotions we felt, but also how it felt having him physically back into our family. I love listening to it, for I know what my dad gave up in order for him to gain his family back, I know it was hard for him, and I know that he now understands what he missed all those years. The song exemplifies everything that my dad was trying to do before he became sober, and now that he is sober. My dad was unable to see how lucky he was in life in having two strong kids and a strong wife. He never understood what it meant to have friends that cared; it was all about him. When he admitted that he was powerless, for the first time he was able to count all his friends on each hand and then some, times one hundred, that had been there all along for him – but he had to "Just Breathe" in order for him to see it.

When he was released from the Prospect House, it was as if my father was breathing for the first time on his own. He did not need machines to make him breathe (alcohol), he did not need others to breathe for him (family members) – he did it on his own. The song *Just Breathe* says just that; slow down, look around, and take in the scenery in front of you, instead of seeing how fast you can get there. It is a formidable lesson in life as my dad saw it, because for all those years leading up to his admittance to the halfway house, Dad was scurrying around trying to please himself, instead of breathing in the fresh air and enjoying life for what it was meant to be.

Like the song says, my dad did not want to hurt anymore. True, his pain was always going to be there, but his destructive pattern of hurting himself and others was stopped in that house. Each day Dad was living was another day in which his pain became more and more bearable; eventually it would no longer exist. The song is also about how our family gave everything they had to my dad's needs, while at the same time my dad was giving nothing back. At the point that he was released from the Prospect House, Dad was giving back, and it proved to him that if you give and expect nothing in return, it will come right back to you through other doors.

If you ever get a chance, look those lyrics up and read them line by line – it is amazing to read those words, for they are so true for everyone, whether an alcoholic or not; just take the time and enjoy life. The denial that had set into Dad's life was a catastrophe, and at that moment in his life he was beginning to settle down to earth. It was a long journey, not only in his life, but in my life as well. I missed my dad for the man that he had been. I missed talking to him about sports, about school, about the Navy and so on. He and I came apart at the hip. It is like placing two people in separate rooms with a glass window. We could see each other, but we were unable to communicate to each other. Seeing him hurting and not being able to help him was the hardest thing a son can do for a father. When he was able to admit his wrongdoing, his life after that changed forever. As I see it, having to move ahead in baby steps every day for the rest of his life is always going to be an obstacle, but an obstacle he is able to overcome when others, including me, have his back.

Mom and Dad's relationship was as strong as ever, and when Dad got out of the Prospect House, Mom welcomed him back into her life. Dad was given strict rules to obey, like those at the halfway house and the Prospect House. Mom's house was going to be run on the same principles. Dad had to attend A.A. meetings, as well as maintain his job. With living on the east side of Cincinnati, Dad was able to transfer department stores and work closer to home. Since my brother and I were out of the house, it was now just Mom and Dad by themselves. For the first time in a long time, they were able to focus on their relationship. Best friends and lovers; that is what they are. I have met many couples who were married, but who were not friends – and that leads to divorce. My parents' marriage was the exact opposite. They were friends all the time; they loved being together no matter what the situation. I remember them as always laughing and happy when Dad was not drinking, and that was how it was going to be again.

A.A. was the center of Dad's recovery, and he was not going to miss it for the world.

12 STEPS OF A.A.

1. We admitted we are powerless over alcohol – that our lives had become unmanageable.
2. Came to believe that a power greater than ourselves could restore us to sanity.
3. Made a decision to turn our will and our lives over to the care of God, as we understand Him.
4. Made a searching and fearless moral inventory of ourselves.
5. Admitted to God, to ourselves, and to another human being the exact nature of our wrongs.
6. Were entirely ready to have God remove all of these defects of character.
7. Humbly asked Him to remove our shortcomings.
8. Made a list of all persons we had harmed, and became willing to make amends to them all.
9. Made amends to such people wherever possible, except when to do so would injure them or others.
10. Continued to take personal inventory and when we were wrong promptly admitted it.
11. Sought through prayer and meditation to improve our conscious contact with God, as we understood Him, praying only for the knowledge of His will for us and the power to carry that out.
12. Having had a spiritual awakening as the result of these Steps, we tried to carry this message to alcoholics, and to practice these principles in all of our affairs.

I had made a reference to the book *Understanding the Twelve Steps*, by Terence T. Gorski earlier, and I want to thank him for writing this book. All these years of being around the disease of alcoholism, the Serenity Prayer, the A.A. meetings, I never understood why my dad was not able to turn his life around. I had seen firsthand that the steps in A.A. do not work – or so I thought. But I sure was wrong. I had to read this book in order to grasp a better understanding of why my dad was able to come clean. Knowledge is what I needed, to understand why and how he was able to be a functional part of our family again.

The 12 Steps are laid out, and if the individual follows them, in order, he will overcome his fears and come out like a champion. That is what my dad did the third time around. Step 5, admit – this is the step that Dad, all those years, was unable to overcome. The first four steps he could accomplish, but step 5 – admitting wrongdoing – was just not going to happen. Denial, like Mr. Gorski says, "is not just a river in Egypt." It is step 5 that got him to step 6, and on to 7 and on and on. His recognition of, and relinquishing of, his denial pattern is the biggest step of his journey. If everyone out there who is an alcoholic were to read the 12 Steps aloud, would they look at those first 5 and say, "That is easy"? My dad did, and when he did that, it all came crumbling down on him.

But at the halfway house and the Prospect House, all the men involved in his journey were there with him. They were the spirits that guided my dad to the light at the end of the tunnel. He was willing to come clean and to confront the facts of his life with men he did not even know. That, to me, is why Dad was able to achieve success in the 12 Steps of A.A. It was not only family that made him quit drinking; it was God who made him quit drinking. Dad turned himself over to God. It was God, with the help of other addicts in a program like no other on the face of the earth. He was not in a high rise with a pool. He was not in a five-star hotel with a gym. He was in a house with sixty beds, a kitchen, and a dining hall that was also the auditorium. He was with men from all walks of life; rich, poor, old, young, highly educated, and no education at all. They looked to each other as brothers and fellow travelers in the journey they were on; they all shared a common quest. That brotherhood meant that each man would help the man next to him, or lead by example. Show and guide others to success, for if you are helping someone else achieve his quest, someone else is helping lead yours, and so the pattern continues over and over. In the book *Winning with People* by John C. Maxwell, he calls it *"The Boomerang Principle."* You throw your efforts towards someone, and for no reason at all those efforts come right back to you through someone else. The whole time that Dad, through his leadership and example, was inadvertently helping others, the men of the Prospect House were helping him, too. *"The Boomerang Principle"* was something that Dad had not practiced for a long time. He could see for the first time that when a person cares for another, expecting nothing in return, that person becomes unselfish. It is all about surviving the storm; the storm is calm sometimes, and is overwhelming other days. But the storm never goes away entirely. With the men, the support, the love, the caring, and the faith of all at the Prospect House and in A.A., Dad was able to come home.

It was June 2002, a few days before Father's Day, when my dad came home to the family. He moved in with Mom and, like I said, their relationship was going to have to come first before anyone else's. Dad and I talked a little, but I knew that in order for him and Mom to hit it off, they needed their space. Mom and Dad began slowly inviting friends over, going out on dates and venturing into their old social life, only this time Dad was not drinking. The remarkable thing about all of this was that my dad's awareness of the disease was rubbing off on other people as well. Sure, people still drank around my Dad, but not like they used to. My dad, I believe was a very valuable tool for others with whom he came into contact. Dad's sobriety rubbed off on them in a positive way. Because he was not drinking, Dad became a huge fan of coffee. His love for coffee had always been tremendous, but since he was not drinking beer, his coffee passion was out of this world. That to me was fine and dandy, as long as he was not drinking.

It was August of 2002 when my employers asked my wife and me to transfer to Indianapolis, Indiana. We jumped feet-first at the idea of moving. For the two years that we had been married, Tarla and I had been through a lot together with my family, and it was the right time to take a chance to move. It also enabled us to find ourselves, without any other strings attached.

Looking back, I thought for a while that our love for each other was going to be affected by my dad's issues. It never was. My wife is a strong woman. Very intelligent, she understands that with marriage comes sacrifice, and she did that the moment she said "yes." Being willing to help with the baggage that came with my family those first two years was a sure sign of her strong love for me. I thank her for going through that two year journey; I thank her for being resilient and accepting my dad for who he is and not for what he was. I thank her for being compassionate to my mom in those two years, and most importantly, I thank her for loving my family. Looking back, some days were just awful, the worst any wife could handle in a new marriage. But she did it and, boy, was she durable. I know it was daunting to her as well as to me in those first two years of marriage, but we got through it with love for family.

We sold our house in two weeks. We moved to the northwest side of Indianapolis, and there our new life would take shape. We even got a house on a golf course; the fairway was right out our back door, and it came with all the free golf balls we could handle. When we moved there, all of our parents drove in from Cincinnati to help us move in. It was just like the Waltons or the Ingalls at a family function, like something out of a movie script. I stood in the master bedroom and looked out the window to the street below. There in the front yard was my dad. I began to get all teary-eyed, for I knew that my wife's and my journey together was just beginning, and his and Mom's journey was beginning as well. I am very proud of my dad's accomplishments, and not for one instant did I ever look down on my dad since he'd moved back into our family. His being in Indianapolis that day was a victory for all. It was a victory for A.A., the halfway house, and the Prospect House. Just having him present in my life was extraordinary. Yes, I was 120 miles away from him now, but that would never keep us apart as long as we still talked.

The year 2002 marked our first winter living in Indianapolis, and that Christmas we went home to spend time with our families. It was a Christmas to remember, for Dad was a part of the celebration, and I was ecstatic that he was there. I could tell that he was just as blissful that my wife and I were there, too.

Time cruised on by those two years; Dad and I talked on a regular basis, about anything and everything, until October of 2004. That month was the greatest month ever invented in the history of months, for on October 19, 2004, our daughter Maggie was born.

Leading up to the due date, my dad and I would reminisce about all the fun things he used to do with me. When I was a child, we would go down to the airport for hours, just to watch the planes land and take off. He would take me to the baseball games that he was coaching, and all the players loved having me around. At the time that my daughter was born, it was as if my dad was going through the stages of new fatherhood right along with me. He would tell me stories of what I did as a kid, and I would listen. We would talk and talk and talk, for I know that being a dad is very important and being a great dad is even more important.

When we brought Maggie home from the hospital, Mom and Dad came out the following week to see her, and it brought great joy to me that my dad was a part of this occasion. When I was watching him with her, seeing how much enjoyment Maggie brought to him, I tried to imagine what it would have been like, had he not been there. What if Dad had succeeded in committing suicide when he'd tried?

But Dad was right there in the moment, holding her, bouncing her on his knee, just like the dad he was. Nothing had changed with him at all, just the fact that now he was sober, and clear of his addiction. The A.A. meetings that he attended allowed him to be there on that day. His success was beyond anything I had ever thought it would be. We have a picture of my mom and dad holding Maggie in their arms, the Grandma and Grandpa they had become together. Not just Grandma, but Grandpa too. If any story were to be written about my dad, that was the one story that had to be shared. With his self-defeating clinging to denial now in his past, Dad was now a grandpa, and he was going to be the best grandpa ever.

There is a movie called *Big Fish*, directed by Tim Burton. In this film, a father is telling his son of all the adventures that he'd had. At the end of the movie, the son carries the father into the water and releases him so that he can die. I remember watching that movie, and it inspired me to call my dad just to say how much I loved him. I was crying really hard, feeling so moved by the film. We talked for over fifteen minutes, and I just kept repeating how much I loved him and how proud I was of him. Those little moments of love and honesty are what kept our relationship strong for all these years.

I always knew I was close to my dad, but to cry to him on the phone was my way of expressing my love to him. Living in Indianapolis, and Dad living in Cincinnati, we were not that far away. But we just never made time for each other to play catch and talk like we used to when I was a kid. I was a little kid crying out for his dad to do something together, just him and me.

In the fall of 2007, I decided that I would take my dad on the utmost, supreme trip. My idea was to create an event that was just for the two of us, one that we could do in three days or less. Sports are always the best route to take with both of us. I knew that his dream had long been to go to the College Baseball World Series. While playing for the University of Cincinnati, his team had missed the chance to play in that event by one series. I was thirty-seven years old and all my life I had heard that story. I knew that if I took him to the 2008 series in Omaha, Nebraska, we would get the chance to see it firsthand together. It was June of 2008 when Dad and I would take our first journey together.

6TH INNING

"I'D WALK THROUGH HELL
IN A GASOLINE SUIT TO PLAY BASEBALL."
– Pete Rose

IT DOESN'T GET ANY BETTER THAN THIS

Baseball is a game that has been in my family's blood since before I was born. It was instilled in my brother's and my brains that baseball was the sport of choice for all of us. Baseball is a game made up of nine innings. It can be boring one minute, and then for the next 20 minutes be the most exciting thing you've ever seen. It is a game where a mediocre player can be on an ESPN highlight reel for the rest of his life with one swing, or one pitch. It is a game that requires patience, outward thinking, guessing, gut instinct, and the stubborn determination to never give up. The team could be down by nine runs in the first inning and come back over the next eight to win the game 10-9. It is a game that strongly resembles life, in that one moment the team is on cloud nine and the next they are scratching their heads because they are behind by 5 runs in the 6th inning.

To me, baseball describes the journey through my relationship with my dad. This chapter is about how we were able to extend a double into a triple, steal home or sit back and wait on a hanging curve and jack it over the left field wall. This, without a doubt, was the trip that took our bond to the next echelon, the next stage. Here we go.

It was the winter of 2007, and I was angry with myself for not having done anything one-on-one with my dad. Yes, I saw him at Christmas, or when he and Mom would drive out to Indiana and spend a day or so with my wife and child and me. But I knew I had to do more than just that. I had to find an opportunity to go and seek what we both needed; being in sync together and sharing thoughts and insights with each other, without anyone else around. I knew I had to be able to share a moment with him, to convey my love for him – and most of all, let him know that I was ecstatic that he was doing so well. So that winter, I invited him to go and see his lifelong dream, the College Baseball World Series, as a Father's Day gift. When I was on the phone with him talking about the idea, I could tell he had a lump in his throat. It was the idea of doing something with his son that his son had heard about his whole life. Like I said, Dad was one series short of going to the World Series with Cincinnati. But now, that series was about to come true for the two of us.

I think back to the time when he was with the University of Cincinnati baseball team, and often marvel at what it must have been like, to be so close to going to the World Series – and yet not make it. I know for a fact that God had a motive for not letting him be there. I am not a very religious person, but for some odd reason, I know now that God had intended that my dad would make that trip with his son. It is a formidable lesson in life, to see your dad at the bottom, drowning in alcohol, and yet see him survive.

It was June 16, 2008. Dad drove into Indianapolis from Cincinnati and arrived at noon. The trip was about to commence, and I was shaking like a leaf on a tree. I was so animated to be going on this trip with him. I'd gotten very little sleep the night before, and here we were, getting ready to take a ten-hour road trip from India-napolis, Indiana to Omaha, Nebraska. All the week previous, I could barely contain my excitement. My wife knew that I was eager. I was bouncing off the walls, cleaning the house; I believe I even gave the dogs a bath before we left. That's not like me, to give them a bath without being told to, but that week I believe that I did. When Dad arrived, I could just tell that this voyage, this road trip was going to be extraordinary; I could see it in his eyes and I knew he could see it in mine.

We loaded up the car, plugged in our GPS, and backed out of the driveway. I put the car in drive and we made it all of 50 feet. I stopped, and said to him "So, you all ready to go?"

He replied, "Jimmy, thank you for asking me to go." We turned the corner and headed south. There was a Starbucks, so in we turned, grabbed two Venti cups of coffee, and off we went.

When I think of Omaha, Nebraska I think of Tom Osborne. I think of cornfields. I think of Warren Buffet, Marlon Brando, Nick Nolte, and Fred Astaire. I think of the University of Nebraska, big farms, and open fields. I think of *why in the heck did the college World Series need to be played in the middle of nowhere? Why not New York, Atlanta, Dallas, San Diego, Chicago? Why did this need to be played in Omaha?* I kept on thinking that as the event got closer and closer. Here it was, a Father's Day gift, and I was driving us out to Omaha to see a baseball game. That was it, Omaha – almost the center of the United States, the NCAA was unselfish in creating the event there, for it is easy for all other 49 states to travel. What a perfect location, easy to get too from all directions – centrally located. Taking others into consideration, before putting themselves first, and that was what this trip was about – Family first, ourselves second.

Baseball. That word in itself describes what our relationship was all about. Baseball is a team sport; it requires nine men and a coach, each of whom must depend on the others to do their jobs. One player is called upon to make a play in the field, just him and only him. Then, he has to throw the ball to the other player, forcing him to make another play. It is a game in which the individual has to be at his best at all times. And it is where team effort is real. In baseball, if you miss the ball on an error and you put a runner on base, the opposing team will probably score a run, or even extend a single hit into a double or triple. That much is true about life as well.

My dad was proof that teamwork is needed every day. But as he was changing his life around, he had to depend on his own actions in order to stay sober. It's the same experience that he'd had at the University of Cincinnati, where Dad played third base. If he made an error, it was his fault, but when he got back in the dugout everyone knew Dad was giving it his best. On the field, he had to keep his head down and his eye on the ball, not thinking about what he had to do next, but thinking in the present; make the play, take two steps towards first, and throw the ball over. Infielders and out-fielders cannot think about the throw they are about to make while the ball is on the way. They need to make the play first, then, with the help of other players relaying the information, the next play will commence. Just as in life, there is a ton of extra weight that we take onto our shoulders, weight we choose to carry instead of discarding it or shaking it off.

My dad and I were teamwork in action. He was the fielder that made the errors in the field, the car was the dugout, and I was the other player patting him on the back. That was what our trip to Omaha was about. It could have been to Paris, Texas, or Paducah,

Kentucky or Battle Creek, Michigan; it did not matter where we were going, but we both knew this was going to be enjoyable.

In 2002, my dad was released from the Prospect House back into society. He was ready to enter the work force full time and he was ready to enter a family that loved him and that he could love. That family was waiting on him with open arms. In the book *The Choice is Yours*, by John C. Maxwell, he has a section called *Lessons I Have Learned about Love*. He has five points. *#5 Love is Unconditional: If there are strings attached, then it isn't really love. A person needs to be loved the most when they deserve to be loved the least. When you love people, you keep loving them. You make their problem, your problem. You stick with them to the end.*

Love is the key ingredient that has made my relationship with my dad so unique. I am in the car with my dad driving, looking around at all the new sights in this part of the United States where I've never driven before, and here I am doing it with my dad, my buddy, the heart and soul of why I have grown up to be a good person. Yes, I have my faults. But I am who I am because of my dad. His strength, his character, his kindness, his morals, his values, made me what I am today. Some he never showed me, but through his addictions, his path has shown me what is important in life. That has made me a better man.

The statement above about unconditional love is exactly what my dad and I had, and will always have, for each other. I have a ton of trophies; I have a ton of awards. I have accomplished so much in my life – yet all of that does not matter to my dad. He loves me for who I am, and that is what I want. My dad has everything that a young son could want in his father. Titles; my dad had them all. President, salesman, booster, coach, neighbor, friend, husband, father, brother, cousin, leader, baseball player – but all of those titles did not matter to me when my dad was homeless and living under the bridge. I wanted him to comprehend that I loved him for who he was, my DAD. He always knew that, but he had to prove to others that he was more than that. The reason was his relationship with his own father. He told me just yesterday on the phone that his dad did not love him unconditionally as far as he could tell; Grandpa was all about the trophies and titles. Dad knew that his father loved him, but it was for all the wrong reasons; the Phillies, University of Cincinnati baseball, semi-pro teams, and all the rest. This trip to Omaha together was exactly what my dad meant when he said "unconditionally." I put our relationship first, to give it the room in which to work out the way that it has. Going to Omaha was no big deal to him. Being with me was the BIG DEAL. That is why the trip was and still is a victory.

A week before we were to take off for Omaha, a huge storm had gone through our route to Nebraska. Iowa was 15 feet under water. We were re-routed on I-70 to St. Louis, then through Kansas City to Omaha. It was no big deal to us, but we knew that would take us six hours out of our way. I had bought tickets in advance for us to see the first game the next day at 1 P.M., so we had 24 hours to get there. We headed west on I-70 from Indianapolis. We were headed for St. Louis first; we had plenty of catching up to do on the trip, and that was what I wanted the trip to be about.

We confronted each other on every single subject known to mankind on that eight-hour drive to Kansas City. The theme we focused our attention on was our love for each other. We talked about how troubling it was not having him at my wedding; he touched on not being able to close on our new house. We talked about him finding God; we talked about me relocating to Indianapolis. We touched on so many topics that it was as if we were out back, playing catch again. The radio was not even on the whole duration of the trip to our hotel. We just loved playing catch-up with each other. That is how our relationship was; we picked up right where we left off. We both knew what had happened in the past, but that was in the past. We were on the outing of our lifetimes, talking about our future together and how pleased we were to be in the present of a future that he and I had both longed for when Dad was going through his separation from alcohol.

There is a web site called ALL PRO DAD (www.allprodad. com) created by Mark Merrill with Tony Dungy. He sends out daily emails called the "Play of the Day." He sends topics of discussion to meditate about all day. One email that really caught my attention was titled "10 things loving fathers do for their children."

1. Loving fathers…love their children's mother.
2. Love them unconditionally.
3. Grow up.
4. Be there.
5. Provide.
6. Discipline.
7. Value education.
8. Raise them to leave.
9. Teach them to take responsibility.
10. Teach them to love this life.

Number 4 *BE THERE* – *"Quality time is all well and good, but it has nothing on Quantity time. Make the time. Everyone has the same 24 hours available. Make yours count."*

When I received this email from the web site, I could not think of anyone more significant than my dad. Be there – be where? It did not matter to my dad at all; he WAS going to be there. Where was everywhere? At my Navy graduation; visiting me in Norfolk, Virginia while I was at school. It was visiting me at my fraternity house at the University of Cincinnati. It was all my baseball games, basketball games, soccer games, and football games. Taking me to college school visits, taking me to Reds games, or Bengals games. It did not matter; he was there for me. It was school functions, school dances; no matter what, I could count on my dad. This is how I saw my dad; always there, always lending a hand in whatever way he could. This is what he gave to me. I love coaching my daughter's softball team; I love going and eating lunch with her at school. I love taking her on vacations; I loved taking her to see Disney World. I love being a driver for my daughter.

My dad showed me how to be there. The 10 items on that list are what my dad did his whole life, every single day while he was living the life of a sober man, one who had control of his priorities. He did it to the best of his ability, day in and day out. Dad was in the car with me, because he had given his heart and soul to becoming the dad, the father, and the husband we wanted him to become again. He was in the car next to me, because of his willingness to put his children first, his loved ones first – *and himself, second.*

Halfway to St. Louis, we had to make our first pit stop. We got gas, and then went over to the fast food chain to grab a bite, planning to get back in the car and go. When we placed our order the cashier asked for my name, and I said, "Steve." Dad looked at me and I looked at him, and we just began to laugh as we took our seats.

Ten minutes later over the intercom I heard, "Order for Steve is up!" He looked at me and we just started to laugh again, this time so hard that we both began to cry. This is what we were doing on our way to Omaha; we were enjoying life, we were who we were, nothing fake. It was a father/son trip that felt like we were driving to Florida for spring break. This is what my dad needed; a good healthy laugh with his son. It was like a pinch on his side, showing him that he was alive and doing so well. It was a "Three Stooges" moment, so funny that when we were together on another trip, Dad used the same name, and we laughed again. Today we still say, "Order for Steve." This corny, corny moment we shared will be with us both forever.

We got back on the highway and off to the races we went. He had an old U.S. map from the 1970s that he brought with him, looking at it as if he was navigating, just like old times. The GPS was on the dash, but Dad had to look at the map to double-check the route on which it was taking us. That was my dad; he'd planned the trip out on the map a few days in advance. He knew we had a GPS, but his old school habits of survival kicked in.

As we came up to the sign that said "St. Louis – 100 Miles," we looked at each other. We each knew what the other was thinking; Cardinals game! I called the Cardinals ticket office, but unfortunately they were out of town, so over the great Mississippi we drove and on to Kansas City we went. It took us eight hours to drive to Kansas City and we were able to get a hotel by the airport. It was very late at night, around 10, so we hit the bed pretty hard after our first day. The next morning, we were up around 6, and my favorite continental breakfast was being provided. As I loaded the car, I told Dad to get a plate and coffee and just relax.

When I came back, he was having a conversation with a complete stranger. I sat down with my plate and he introduced me as his son, Jim, as if he had known this person for a long, long time. This was my dad; he could be knee-deep in quicksand and he would take the time to get to know the person rescuing him before he would allow them to help him. I guess that is where I got my side of the "A" personality. Believe me, it is so much fun to talk to strangers. Some of the best conversations I have had were with the staff at museums, and the lunch ladies at my child's school. Well, off we went; we had a three-hour drive ahead of us, from Kansas City to Omaha, so we could not waste any more time.

As we drove away from Kansas City and headed north on I-29, I just looked at him, appreciating him for who he was now. Like I said, he'd spent so much of his life futilely searching for some ever-more-important adventure to try and confirm something about his value to others. Now, here he was in the car being himself, being who he was intended to be.

I loved the fact that he and I only had three more hours to go until we were in Omaha, and this was when the communication line opened for the first time in our relationship, on a topic that I had been hoping for a long time we could talk about. We talked about all the great players and the great coaches who had participated in the College World Series. We talked about his coach, Glenn Sample, at Cincinnati. My dad had total respect for this man, who later went on to be the official score keeper of the Cincinnati Reds. He saw in this man a father, a mentor – someone by whose example he wanted to live own life. But unfortunately, instead of my dad living out his dreams, he had to live out *his* dad's. Being a salesman was a respectable job for him, but he was born to be a coach, a teacher, a mentor, a leader, and he was never given the opportunity to do so. Here he was, 60 years old, a recovering alcoholic, sitting in my car talking about all the things he could have done if someone had just supported him in his dreams. I remember him opening up as I just sat there and listened to him talk for an hour or so on the topic of dreams.

It hit me hard to listen to him talk of his relationship with his dad; his mom had been the supportive one. But in the '50s, women really did not have a strong voice in the house. Grandpa, his dad, was king of the house. Listening to my Dad, agreeing with him, supporting him, was what this trip was intended to be about, and we got our money's worth in those thirteen hours from Indianapolis to Omaha. I had never heard my dad disclose anything of that kind to me in the history of our relationship. But I was 37 and he was 60. That is when it dawned on me that denial had set into his relationships with everyone with whom he'd come into contact, his whole life up until now. It took my dad 37 years to reveal a side of himself to me that he had been yearning to share.

It was now that I got a glimpse of a man who had come full circle in his life, and was finally able to share that with his friends. I was that friend, and I felt significant and very fortunate to be the one there to listen to him share his grief with me. I just wished that he had done this sooner, but beggars cannot be choosers, and I was no chooser. I just loved him being in the car with me, loved him being able to share feelings with me, and loved him being able to feel comfortable in communicating with me. Him being there and feeling safe with me was how we were victorious in his road to recovery.

In his book *What are You Living For?*, the author Pat Williams has a passage that says, *"Our enemy never gives us any rest; the battle goes on and on – but it is a good battle, and worth fighting."* That is exactly how I saw my dad. It was a battle for him to explain his demons to me, it was a battle for him to overcome alcoholism, and it was a battle for him not to be at my wedding. But Dad's battle had only just begun; he has to fight every day for the rest of his life for the relationships that he wants. He has to defeat the enemy (alcoholism) every single day, one step at a time. Some days, I'm sure, are easier than others, but his family is the reason for his battle with the enemy. The fight against alcoholism is a fight that he is willing to confront. He has his scars and his wounds, but he keeps getting up. Round after round he keeps fighting; like a prizefighter, he never gives in and never quits.

The University of Cincinnati baseball team has never made it to the Baseball College World Series, although they have come very close. Kevin Youkilis of the Boston Red Sox came close. Sandy Koufax, with all his wins, surely did come close. My dad was one series away from getting there. He hit the game-winning homerun to get them to the next series, but they lost the next series. And here it was, 41 years later that he was pulling into Omaha with me at the helm.

When we entered the city limits of Omaha, I could tell he was getting very eager, because he was getting very fidgety. I could tell he was thinking back to what it would have been like to enter the city limits with all the teammates who he'd cherished. He appreciated all the guys on his team that he played with at Cincinnati. He still talks about them as if they see each other often, but he has lost track of them. (I hope some of them will see this, and look him up and talk to him, and I will encourage my dad to look you guys up as well.) As we headed west from I-29 to I-80, looking around and stargazing, we came up on the exit for the stadium. We got off and headed south on 13th Street and sure enough, there on the left side of the street was the shrine of all stadiums; Rosenblatt Stadium (the Blatt).

Dad and I have been to many stadiums; Riverfront, Veterans, Three Rivers, Candlestick and others. But this to us was the most distinguished of them all. This 23,145-seat stadium is where young college men come for the chance to be called College Baseball World Champions. This sports soil is where teamwork, hard work, dreams, vision, and excellent footwork all come together. This ground could tell a great story for every year it's seen, going back for many. The first World Series game was played in the stadium in 1950, and it was the site for all the subsequent series games through 2010. This stadium is where fans from all around the country come and applaud their team to victory; it is where men turn a ball and a bat into something of significance. It is where young boys all over the country dream of playing, taking the stage, putting their name in the books as having been there.

The Bearcats were so close; just one more series, and they were in. Although as a team they won many games that year, they did not make it to Omaha. My whole life I had heard that story many, many times. I never thought the day would come when I would get the chance to catch a glimpse of a game with my dad here in Omaha. Looking back was not an option for us anymore. Someone once said that the rearview mirror in the car is so small for a reason; you're only meant to look back long enough to catch a glimpse. Keep your eyes forward on the windshield, for everything you need is ahead. That was it; this trip was about looking forward, not back. The past was gone, the slate wiped clean.

SOPHOMORE JIM SERGER hit a pinch-hit home run with two men on in the seventh inning of the third (8-7) game. That cut the score from 7-3 St. Louis to 7-4 and gave the Bearcats the big lift they needed. They went on to score two in the 8th to win.

Looking at this photo, you get an idea of how my dad looked in 1967. This photo was taken when he hit that 400-foot homerun to get to the next game. When his dad passed away in 2008, this photo and the article were found in his dad's dresser drawer. That day, I'm sure, was tremendously important to my dad, because he discovered that his own father had thought so much of his achievement that he chose to keep this memento of it next to his bed until his death. Is that love? Yes, it is. Is it *unconditional* love? No, it is not.

His dad loved him, but he never told him that in public. He never kissed or hugged him, never let him know that he loved him for who he was. He had the article to prove that his son hit the homerun, to show that his son was a trophy to him. My dad never, ever did that to me. This trip was about unconditional love. It was about him believing in me, and me believing in him. It was about a father and son duo that was living the dream of togetherness. It was about us seeing something for the first time, experiencing it as a team – just like the Bearcats baseball team would have done. The year was 2008, 41 years later, but that didn't matter to him or to me. He is a winner, and just seeing him looking at the stadium as we drove up to it was like a miracle for me, as it was for him.

In an email that I received from *All Pro Dad*, the "Play of the day" was *10 ways to integrate sports with a family*. Out of all 10 I thought the most of *#4 – The Real Thing*. It was exactly what my dad and my family had been doing for years as I was growing up. It was one thing to watch an event on TV. But it was another to be there in person. The College World Series was just like that. My parents had taken me to many Reds games, and plenty of Bengals games, live and in person. We'd gone to the circus, the fair, Taste of Cincinnati, Kings Island, Coney Island, River Downs horse track, balloon launches early in the morning, to Lake Michigan, to Florida, and to Disney World. My parents always did their best to make the event The Real Thing. It was Christmas Eve 1994, when I first made the trip back to Cincinnati from Japan, that my parents took my brother and me to the Cincinnati Bengals game. Wow, what a nice gift that was. Here they were, with very little money, and they got us good seats and paid for everything. That is who they were. They wanted to give us a memorable experience as a family, and we had that together. That is what my dad and I had there in Omaha – The Real Thing.

We drove down 13th Street and parked the car behind some guy's house. The guy charged us all of five dollars. I said we were seeing a double header – should we pay $10? He said "Sure," and my dad looked at me and just laughed. He knew what I did was right, but how many other people would have paid twice because they were seeing two games? The guy would have been fine with five dollars – but that wouldn't have felt right to me. We walked out from behind the guy's house, and there it was, right in front of us on the other side of the street – *The Blatt!* The crowd was huge; kids running around, dads and sons holding hands. Dads were walking, pointing out everything they could see to their little guys. Vendors were hawking shirts; food stands were selling food and handing out complimentary drinks. Music was playing; you could hear the intercom system from inside, "Test one, two, and three." The sights and sounds are what make an event so spectacular – and we were right in the middle of it. It was 10 A.M., and already the place was electric; you could just feel the excitement beaming off my dad's face. Here we were at the center of college sports to him, and he was with his son.

We walked up to the main entrance and there was a huge line. I had to get tickets to the next game, which was at 6. I told Dad to hang out up there, and I would walk down and wait in line for the tickets. As I got closer and closer to the booth I heard air brakes being applied, and I saw that there were two commercial buses that had just parked next to the entrance. A good-sized crowd hovered around, and out came the LSU Tigers baseball team. Looking up at the crowd, I found my dad in two seconds. He was right in the middle of the crowd, clapping for a team he had read about a few days ago, for being in the big game.

I got closer to the window and I grabbed two for the next game, then ran up to see the next bus pulling in. Sure enough, it was Rice University, pulling in right behind the other two buses. I stood next to Dad and he looked at me as the players exited the bus and said, "It does not get any better than this" – he knew this was the moment, he knew this is what it was all about. It was all about the men coming off the bus. He knew his whole life was at a complete standstill. It gave me goose bumps to watch, and I almost started to cry.

Here my dad was 61 years old, and he was acting like a 20 year-old. It was awesome, unbelievable to see him gleaming with such admiration for those players. I could tell by his posture that he was reminiscing about what it would have been like to take that step off the bus as a Cincinnati Bearcat. Instead, he grabbed me and told me, "Thanks." I knew it was all about him and me that day. But it sure felt good to see him think about his glory days. That part of him is what father/son relationships are about. You share those archives with your son/daughter and you let them envision what it could have been like, right alongside you.

It was 11, and we entered the stadium. Not too many people were in there yet, so we rushed down behind home plate and just sat there, seeing, pointing, talking, laughing, and sharing our impressions of the stadium together. We watched both teams take batting practice. He talked about the stadium's history, and we talked about the records of the teams we were about to watch, Rice vs. LSU, and Owls vs. Tigers. We got up and walked over to our seats 20 rows back, right between first base and right field. Perfect seats, perfect day, perfect everything. Right in front of us was the nicest family from Louisiana, a father, son, daughter and wife, all decked out in LSU attire. The stickers, pompoms, and the jerseys were ready to go. I had on a Miami Hurricanes baseball shirt and my dad was wearing his University of Cincinnati baseball shirt. As the game was getting ready to commence, we looked at each other and said, "Thanks." It was unbelievable to be there in that moment with him.

It is kind of weird that when I was looking up the history of the College World Series, I found out that my dad's favorite president played in the first World Series. President George H.W. Bush played for Yale in 1947, the same year my dad was born. President Bush played first base for Yale, and in that game they played the University of California. California won that game. Yale had beaten the odds; the little Ivy League school made it to the big time. Even though they lost, they gained tremendous respect for what they had achieved in sports as a *team*.

Here my dad and I were, watching something super together, and believing in something greater than us. We both knew that this never would have come to pass, had I not continued believing in my dad while he was a bottom feeder. Dad was very sick those years when he was at rock bottom; very, very, very sick. He should have never even been at that game with me. The odds of him making it there were, I believe, about ten million to one. Yes, he still had a chance – but those chances were very slim. Alcohol is a very addictive substance, and it almost killed our family. It took all of my family to believe in him, and it took my dad to believe in himself. Being in that stadium was the highlight of our travels. We were way down in the valley years before, and now we were on the highest peak. Climbing Mt. Everest is the way I see it. It took many teams, stations, and base camps to get us to the pinnacle – but we did it, and those two seats were proof that you must never quit on a loved one if they are willing to walk with you.

Go the distance – just like in *Field of Dreams*. Kevin Costner's character was told to go the distance. He did not know where that was taking him, but at the end, when it was just him and his dad playing catch, he knew that going the distance had paid off. Everyone was against him, but his vision and his actions proved everyone wrong. Just like my dad; we proved to him that he was wrong, that he could quit drinking and he could *go the distance*.

Here it was, high noon. The first game of the double header and the two teams, Rice and LSU, were ready to take center stage. We sat there and enjoyed the whole game. We ate chips, hot dogs, and even snuck out to get some ice cream. The game was unbelievable. We were rooting for Rice in the first inning just because we loved their coach, Wayne Graham. But as the game went on, we were no longer rooting for any particular team, we were cheering for all of the athletes down on the field. All the fans around us were doing the same thing. They were rooting and clapping at every great play, hit, walk, and bunt. It did not matter to most fans which team was winning – what mattered to them and us was just being there, taking in the atmosphere. That is what our relationship was – it was great company, great atmosphere. We could have been hunting in Alaska, or skeet shooting, or fly-fishing, or just sitting in the family room talking. It did not matter to us; he with me and I with him was a win/win!

The game was over and we left the park. When we went out front, there were all sorts of entertainments offered for us to choose from. Instead, we found a tree and sat in the shade to relax. We sipped on a few bottles of water – it was hot that day. Dad puffed on his cigar and we just sat there and talked it up some more. We began talking to others who were just passing by, as though we were sitting on the front porch 30 years ago. Dad had a kind word for everyone going by. He struck up so many conversations, and it was fun learning where everyone had come from. He was in his comfort zone; baseball was also in that zone, and his son was in that zone. His game face was on, just like when he was making the starting lineup for the little league team. He was in it from the word go.

We headed back into the park for the second game. This time, our seats were on the third base side. Way up in section X, we had the last two seats in the upper right hand corner. Once again, these seats were great. No one behind us, and Dad was at the top of the steps, so he could stretch his legs out in the aisle. Sitting in front of us was a young father and his daughter. To the right of us was another young man with his dad. Of course, we began to talk to them as well. The guys to the right told us that they flew up every year from Florida to watch the games. The young dad and daughter lived in Omaha and were starting a family tradition by going to the game. This was not just a game any longer. The days leading up to our trip, it had just been a game – but being there, it was an event, an opportunity for people to see that dreams do come true. It was an event that built character, built relationships; it was an opportunity to have meaningful conversations. It was where the *game of catch* was played throughout the day. It was where tradition rewarded the individual for hard work and determination in competition.

It is an experience that happens in backyards all over the country; it is an experience that is so meaningful that you feel the warmth inside you. You feel the sun on your face, the cool breeze on your back. You hear the sound of the bat, the cheers of the fans, and the smell of hotdogs. It feels like an all-American moment.

This ticket is living proof that you can make any dream come true; you just have to believe in yourself, your team, your teachers, your coaches, or your wife. When my dad held this ticket in his hand, it was proof to him that the moment was real. It is like talking up a big game, and then doing something about it. This little piece of paper was bigger than life itself, for it exemplified every moment of success that he had had in his life.

In the book *Think Like a Champion* by Donald J. Trump, he states that, *"Champions go the extra mile. We all know when we've done enough and when we've really exerted ourselves. Make an effort to exert yourself – every day."* This is a trenchant statement as applied to my dad's life. For all of those years leading up to his addiction recovery, Dad had not exerted himself to be a champion. He talked up a big game, but this time he had to go the extra mile. If he was to survive, he had to exert himself every single day, and for the rest of his life. The addiction that he has could come back to haunt our family again in the future. But this time, he is thinking like a champion. He is thinking of others before himself, and that ticket stub is proof that he has worked and will continue to exert himself every day. The ticket is comparable to an award given to knights for bravery in medieval times. It is like the Navy Cross awarded to the Navy SEAL for putting his team first, instead of himself. What this ticket means to my dad and me is beyond anything that I can describe. It is achievement; it is triumph.

Sitting there in Section X for the second game, we were able to watch the University of North Carolina and Fresno State University. Once again, we were not just watching the game; we were soaking it in like a sponge. The game started at 6 P.M. and we were able to watch the game under the lights. It was exciting as the sun set and the lights came on. The two teams battled it out, but Fresno State won the game. In fact, they would go on to win the College World Series that year. In the double-header, we got to see three World Series championship teams: LSU (2009), Rice (2003) and, of course, Fresno State.

As I sat there with my dad and we went through the programs together, we talked about how he'd coached all those years in Little League baseball. He said he would stay up 'till two in the morning putting together a lineup, putting the kids at the right positions, thinking about the starting pitcher and the reliever (who was also the starting right fielder, or short stop). We looked at the names of the coaches for all four of the teams we saw that day: Wayne Graham (Rice), Paul Mainieri (LSU), Mike Fox (North Carolina), and Mike Batesole (Fresno State). What I saw in those four coaches I saw in my dad that day – I saw a side of him that I had not seen since I was a little kid, and that was the love of the game of baseball. It was not the fact he played and coached baseball. It was the kids he coached that he loved, especially my brother and me, and his generosity and enthusiasm in sharing what he knew and loved was tremendous. My dad loved the game of baseball because he loved people. That is baseball, to me. That is my dad, to everyone.

After the game was over, we left the park and headed for the car. It was 10 P.M., and we had to get on the road so that we could make it home the next day at a decent time. We got back on I-29 and headed north. Dad had called AAA, and the roads through Iowa had reopened, which saved us four hours of driving. So we drove I-80 east all the way to Des Moines, Iowa. We stopped at 2 A.M. to grab some shut-eye, and all the way home we talked about the two games. We could not believe we had driven eleven hours and had seen a double-header, and now we were in Iowa getting ready to sleep. We laughed so hard at how crazy we were to do so much in so little time, but it sure was worth it.

Up and at 'em at 8 and off through Iowa City, down through Champaign, Illinois, we would go. I was tired of driving and I asked Dad if he would drive, and sure enough, without any hesitation, he jumped right at the helm. A few hours later, we were crossing the Indiana state line. Dad turned the radio on to ESPN. We had not listened to the radio one time the whole ride out and three quarters of the way back, but that is a sign of one heck of a road trip, if you ask me. We came to the Indianapolis city limits and headed north to Carmel on I-465. I was back at the wheel and, as we neared home and the end of our adventure, our emotions rose again. It was hard for us to end the trip, but we both knew that we had many more trips together ahead of us. Fifty-plus hours, a double-header in Omaha, and lots of catching up were coming to a close. But as we pulled into my driveway, we both knew it was an accomplishment, the voyage of a lifetime. It was the most memorable experience I'd ever had with my dad. I'd known many great days with him – but that one was the icing on the cake.

This picture shows what I wanted to achieve, and we did it.

As we were finishing this chapter, I asked him what was the best part about the College World Series trip for him. He responded, "Jimmy, being with you was all that I wanted in life. That trip proved that I loved you and you loved me."

What else can a son ask for? My dad loves me, not my trophies – *me*. As I talk to my dad now, I hear something in his voice that was missing in his addiction days, and that is putting other people first. My dad is the best coach I have ever had, and he is the best mentor I have ever been around, and I have been around very successful mentors. My dad is my friend, my buddy, and the person I would love to be – now that he is sober again.

7TH INNING

"GOD, I JUST LOVE BASEBALL."
– Robert Redford in *The Natural*

EXTREME DREAMS DO COME TRUE

Pat Williams, Senior Vice President of the Orlando Magic, wrote a book called *Extreme Dreams Depend on Teams.* The enjoyment I got out of the book was far greater than I'd thought it could be; the book touched on the College Baseball World Series, Fresno State and the hurdles that they had to conquer in order to win it. This was the same College World Series that Dad and I had attended together as a team. Those hurdles and obstacles are what my dad and I had to overcome. More importantly, it was the teamwork and the vision that put my dad and me back on the winning team. With everything that we have gone through together, that book made me reflect on our shared journey, and reminded me to be grateful that Dad was alive.

When I was done with the book, I called him on the phone and told him all about it. I made my mom go out and purchase it, and today that is the only book that he has read in over 5 years. The whole time when my dad was going through his recovery stage, it took many teams to transform him for the better; me, my wife, my brother, my mom, the halfway house, and the Prospect House. The only thing that got him on the team is the fact that he came clean with his drinking problem. That was the only event in his transformation to sobriety that did not require a team. His team had been rooting him on all these years, but he was not listening, and he was thrown off the team for lack of hustle, so as to speak. After admitting that he had a drinking problem, Dad was entering the minor leagues (just like he'd always wanted), except this time it was A.A. This was going to be his league forever, and there was no more going back down or going way up, because this is the league of a sober man.

In 2009, I took him to the U.S. Senior Golf Open here in Carmel, Indiana for a Father's Day gift. My wife bought me a seven-day pass to go to the event. I called my dad and said "This is going to be another moment for you and me to be with each other, one on one, and enjoy each other's company." He arrived at the house at 7 A.M., and by 8 we were on the golf course. It was unbelievable, and not too hot; it was just right to watch all the golfers that he watched when he was my age, and I was able to enjoy it with him.

Lenny Watkins, Tom Watson, Greg Norman – the list went on and on. The look on Dad's face told me that he was on cloud nine. Here we were, watching and chasing his idols down just to watch them hit or putt. As I looked over at him, I realized that this was no longer a dream; this was real. Just to have my dad next to me, putting his arm around me, saying he loved me and thanking me for inviting him, was wonderful. I love these moments together, just him and me with no one else around. We talk about my family, job, his health, sports, politics, Mom – everything under the sun. Just looking at him and expressing our interest in each other is all I want, and we have that.

All my life, I have heard the story about his having been selected by the Philadelphia Phillies. He is so proud of that moment, and to this day he still remembers the scout inviting him to the Phillies organization. Everyone that knew Dad personally had heard this story, but not too many people outside of the family were even aware of his having been selected. In 1965, between his senior year of high school and his freshman year of college, Dad was playing in what was called Class "A" amateur league. That is where the head coach of the Glendale Serve-All Electric Baseball Team, Richie Stephens, came into contact with my dad. Mr. Stephens was also a minor league scout for the Philadelphia Phillies. He was a scout for the greater Cincinnati area, which included Kentucky, Indiana and Ohio. That summer Mr. Stephens sent a letter to Dad's house letting him know that the Phillies would like to offer him a contract. On receiving the letter, Grandpa of course said "no," for it would have meant Dad losing his draft deferment, as I said earlier.

Every year since our trip to Omaha to watch the World Series, I have planned out what we should do next. I think up crazy ideas. Parachuting, renting a car and driving up and down the West Coast; just anything that he and I can do together to strengthen our relationship and to let him know that I support and love him. I looked up the baseball schedule for the Phillies and the Reds (his two favorite teams) and saw that the Phillies were playing a game Saturday night at 7 in Philadelphia, against the Florida Marlins. Then I saw that on Sunday afternoon, the Reds were playing the Pittsburgh Pirates in Pittsburgh. I called him up and said, "We can go see two games, but we will have to be back Sunday night so I can be at work Monday morning." So, in the spring of 2010, I lined up the plans for yet another Father's Day gift.

Once again, we were off to another sporting event. I spent the night at my parents' house, and we were up at 5 A.M. It would take twelve hours to get to Philly from Cincinnati, and we were all packed and ready to go. Mom made us coffee and sandwiches, and a ton of snacks. We were off to the place that had chosen him to play ball, the place that I had dreamed of seeing him play. I knew that our dream was to become reality, and that we were going to do this as a team.

Twelve hours later, we were entering the park, and our eyes were as big as grapefruit. We were like two little kids in a candy store. I took his picture in front of the Steve Carlton statue. We sat in center field and ate dinner at the restaurant, and just talked and talked until 6:30. Then we ventured over to our seats. Our seats were ten rows behind home plate. It was so cold that night, but it did not even matter. We drank so much coffee that I believe they ran out of it in the section where we sat. We loved the Philly Phanatic mascot; we loved the crowd. We loved everything about it, except the fact that no one had hit a homerun. Would nobody light up the homerun light and ring the bell? It was bottom of the ninth, and Jayson Werth was up to bat. Sure enough, he hit a homerun, and the bell in center field lit up the ballpark, and the bell rang. We looked at each other and gave each other high fives, for we knew that we as a father/son combo had hit the homerun in our relationship. It was as if God was saying, "You two have come so far in your relationship. Here is one for your hard work. Keep it up, there's a lot more to come."

We left the park at 11 P.M., and headed west towards Pittsburgh. We had two diet Cokes and one Sprite left in our reserve, along with one box of pretzels. We drove until 2 A.M., then pulled over and got a hotel, just laughing and carrying on about the home run, the game, and the atmosphere. It was awesome. My dad had only dreamed this occasion would come, and here I was able to go with him, and to somehow reward him for being a great father. So many years he had been driving me to games, practice, dances – so many events and activities. And now, I was driving him. Needless to say, we were riding on excitement. We'd been together nearly twenty-four hours between the car and the game, but it did not matter to us. We were on a mission.

The next morning, we headed for Pittsburgh. We arrived at noon, and the game was at 1, so we parked and went to our seats. It was a little overcast and drizzling a bit. But it did not matter. The crowd compared to the night before was way down, maybe 15,000 at best. Then again, the Penguins were in the finals, so the locals had more to cheer for that day. It did not bother Dad and me one bit. We sat in the club level right behind home plate and just took in the whole moment. We could see Marty Brennaman behind us calling the game for the Reds on 700 WLW Radio; it was just good to be there with Dad. We watched the game, and Jay Bruce hit two homers that day. The Reds lost that game, but it really did not matter to either one of us. As a team, Dad and I won a little victory for Team Serger.

The game was over around 5, and off for Cincinnati we went. It was another six-hour drive, but time flies when you are having a good time. We kept saying, "We are two wild and crazy guys," just like Steve Martin and Dan Aykroyd. We were in it to win it, and win it we did. That night, we got back around 11 P.M., and Mom came out to see us as we got in. She loved having Dad back; they hugged and kissed, and we told her all about it. She even made us sandwiches; here it was so late and she had waited up for us, just to welcome us back safely.

As I jot these sentences down, I know that he was meant to be my dad. I remember many a time when I did not think I was ever going to see my dad again. People search for their reason in life and never find it; my dad did that many years ago. He kept searching and searching. He would find something, and then go out on another quest, not knowing that his quest was already fulfilled, the quest of being a dad – a great, loving dad, one whose example would guide me on my quest to be a great dad.

The true reason I am writing this book with my dad is to add another baby step to our relationship. I take these trips with him to help us mend our sorrows and strengthen our characters. It helps us to talk about our relationship, and through this book we are able to express our love, our concern and our willingness to forgive. It is not a fast process at all. I still think back to what he did to our family, and note that this will never happen to mine. I feel as if he was put on this earth to spread the word of his success to other people. He is never one to brag, but with me he always has. I talk about my dad all the time, all for good reasons, just as he does about me. Yes, in the past my dad and I did not see eye to eye, but with the grace of God he and I are trying our best to mend that relationship.

In the book *Mr. Little John's Secrets to a Lifetime of Success* by Pat Williams, he says, *"Whatever mistakes you made in the first half of your life, you can recover – if you start the second half with patience."* Patience is exactly what it has taken with my dad and me. It took almost six years to engage him to go and do something together; I had to see firsthand that my dad was going to stay on track, that he would not just talk about standards, but live up to them. As I've said, he has always been a salesman, but those days are long gone. Now he is a dad. Patience has taught him well, just as Luke Skywalker learned from Yoda. Patience is what got Dad to Omaha and to the U.S. Open, to Pittsburgh and Philly. But those were rewards for our many years of patience. Patience is what got Dad from homeless, to halfway house, to Prospect House, and back into Mom's house. Patience is how Dad and I harnessed our energy in our growing relationship.

Seeing my dad through the time that he entered Prospect House all the way to seeing him the way he is today is the product of *patience*. He always wanted more, and was never satisfied with what he had. At Prospect House, he had nothing, and that was great. He had to get his life back in order, and he was going to do it, no matter how long it took. Patience is the driving force to keeping him healthy and sober. He and I talked about his demons, his health, and his understanding on all of our trips. This is an avenue that he and I drive down every time we talk. We share a lot of information on the road trips, but the information that is expressed the most is our love for one another. I could never imagine him not being around anymore. That day will come in the future, and I will accept that day, but 20 years ago in 1990 I was not ready to lose him. Again in 1999, I was not ready to lose him.

Here it is 2011, and another venture in our lives is starting to come to fruition. Just last week, I spent the night at Mom and Dad's house so we could start to put this book together. We bounced many ideas off of each other. I even had to teach him how to use a laptop computer, so that he could take what he had written down and put it into some kind of form. We just kept on laughing and laughing about the book, and the funny stories that we should add, then the funny stories that we should not add; the great times we had growing up together, the memories, the passion and the zest we had for one another in our father/son relationship. It was the first time in a long time that he and I were not using sports as a background against which to express our love. We just sat up and talked like a father and a son, without any destination involved. We didn't require any activities as icebreakers any longer. Just to have him in the same room with me was more than enough for me. That is our relationship now; we both are in this together, one day at a time. People say that time will heal all wounds, and I would have to agree. Each day that goes by, I feel more excited about my Dad's progress. I see it in his eyes. The willpower that he has shown, the commitment that he is giving, is that of someone who wants to keep the game going into extra innings.

It is bottom of the ninth, the bases are loaded, and my dad is up to bat. Two outs and the winning run on first, he hits a triple and the game is over. He is jumped on at third base, and everyone around him is patting him on the back. He is crying, he is so ecstatic that he got the hit and won the game.

Well, Dad, let me tell you firsthand that the game has been won. I am one of the many people there at your side, telling you what a great job you have done. I am so proud to be your son; I would not trade the past experiences for anything. You have shown me as well as many others that anything can be achieved, if you want it badly enough. Life is hard, and I will be the first to admit that. In my Dad's case, his life is showing me that extreme dreams do come true. Life gives us extra innings all the time; it is up to us to take advantage of them. Do not waste time. Have a map; plan it out. Patience will get you to where you want to go, and with God leading the way, all things are possible.

If you use a search engine on my dad's name, this is what you will find on the internet:

Addict waits five months for treatment

Jim Serger had a family, a good job and was by all societal standards a success, until alcoholism and depression took control of his life. Following a suicide attempt and loss of everything of value – his family, friends and reputation – Jim landed at the Mount Airy Shelter for homeless men.

He attended regular A.A. meetings and realized he needed intensive treatment before re-entering the workplace. **The Prospect House** was the answer, with its intensive program and high success rate. Jim spent five months on the waiting list and was fortunate to get a placement where a solid framework for sobriety has been laid out for him. Many addicts relapse while waiting for residential treatment. Fortunately, Jim was successful and currently resides at Prospect House.

It is astonishing that this article is all that is written of my dad. However, I believe this article to be the supreme assessment of all of his achievements. The way I see it, this article is a small, yet very powerful piece, in that it proves that when one person is willing to accept responsibility, anything is attainable in life. We hear about individuals giving up all the time, and they never truly see that they were just a few steps away from achieving greatness. Mickey Mantle was sent down to the minor leagues, and he called his dad up and said that he was not meant to make the majors. His dad said "Hang in there," and sure enough, he went on to become one of the greatest baseball players of all time. One piece of aspiration and stimulation is all it takes to get one over the hump. That is what my dad did. The key word in the article is *successful* – which is also winning, victorious, triumphant, unbeaten, flourishing, thriving, booming. This is how he was able to go back home to our house in the end. He had won the game.

This is living proof that any obstacle can be overcome.

- Living proof that addiction can be overcome.
- Living proof that halfway houses work.
- Living proof that the Prospect House works.
- Living proof that counseling works.
- Living proof that A.A. works.
- Living proof that priests and pastors are needed.
- Living proof that denial can be thrown out.
- Living proof that relationships can be won again.
- Living proof that LOVE will prevail in the end.
- Living proof that when you invite God into your life, He will come.

This is living proof that sometimes weird, crazy, trips are still a part of life, even if you're sixty-three years old. My dad was acting as if he was on a spring break trip – showing himself and the world that he was alive.

As I look at these two photos, one of him in Philly and one of him in Pittsburgh, I cannot help feeling overjoyed at the goofiness of his smile. He was so funny when I was taking these. He was an adult, but more of the little kid inside of him was shining through. He was so happy to have taken this trip with me, and I with him as well.

In twenty years, I will be sixty years old and he will be eighty. Many more goofy trips and fun memories to be made are ahead of us. But one day he will be gone. I think and hope that when it comes, I will be ready to handle that day. But in reality, nobody is ever really ready to lose someone whom they love, and I know that I will miss my dad when he goes. I love him, I respect him, and most importantly I got to enjoy being with him – because I made the time to be with him. I made time to go the distance, in order to play catch.

This book in your hands today has made our relationship stronger than it had been in the past eleven years. This book is what my dad and I gave each other for Father's Day, 2011. Even if it's never published, we will still have made our relationship stronger through the writing of it, and that is the gift we wanted. We talk every day, sometimes twice a day. I spent the night at his house three times to go over the book. Since we started this book back in December of 2010, we have made strides on the communication side of our relationship, sharing feelings on topics that we used to avoid. We have been able to share deep thoughts with each other about how we felt while Dad and I were going through the pain of his alcoholism. This book is about our sheer devotion to each other over the past eleven years. Like I said, we do not need a sports venue to share our thoughts anymore; we just needed to realize that for the first time in our lives together, our love for each other is strong, and that is what made this book happen. For if unconditional love was not there, this voyage would have never been completed. I love you, Dad.

8TH INNING

"WHEN A FATHER GIVES TO HIS SON,
BOTH LAUGH; WHEN A SON GIVES TO HIS
FATHER, BOTH CRY."
– William Shakespeare

DAD'S CHAPTER

This book has been a very difficult exercise for me. I am so proud of Jimmy for his hard work and dedication to the project, and overwhelming work was humbled by the outpouring of love. His description of the unconditional love that overcame all obstacles is absolutely true, and works both ways, "unconditionally." I am very fortunate that this same unconditional love also applies to my wife and best friend Marilyn, our youngest son Andy, and other family and friends mentioned in the book. Without them, my recovery might never have happened. That said, the title of the book *Go the Distance*, is certainly appropriate. A father/son relationship is never-ending, and takes the commitment of both parties to realize its potential. The early years, of course, are a father's responsibility. Writing this book was a painful reminder to me of how my selfishness very nearly lost all of those I love, forever. I did not do my part, and had not God intervened, through the guidance of Alcoholics Anonymous, the Prospect House, and Mount Airy Shelter, I would not be with my family today.

Alcoholics are selfish to the core, and that is the essence of the disease. It's a deceptive mental illness, which deprives you of rational thinking and replaces it with self-pity and self-centered emotional perceptions. Only through belief and trust in a higher power and the practice of the 12 Steps can the alcoholic escape "self-center," live a productive life, and be helpful to others. We must do it every day and re-commit to our powerlessness – every day. A.A. teaches us how to recognize when we are slipping before we take the next drink, and get back on track.

I've been alcohol-free for 12 years at the time of the writing, but that's not good enough! The old "self-pity" and "unworthiness" have crept back as I've recently started a new job and I am feeling very inadequate. It's made it more difficult (very selfish) to remember what I had become during writing this book. Celebrating the joyous relationship I have with Jimmy is easy and should be my only focus.

My dedication to this book is to "shake it off," concentrate on my *gratitude first*, and be the person that God, A.A., Jimmy, Andy, Marilyn, and I know that I can be.

The 3rd Step Prayer of A.A. is my Motto:

**GOD, I OFFER MYSELF TO THEE,
TO BUILD WITH ME,
AND TO DO WITH ME AS THOU WILL.
RELIEVE ME OF THE BONDAGE OF SELF,
THAT I MAY BETTER DO THY WILL.
TAKE AWAY MY DIFFICULTIES,
THAT VICTORY OVER THEM MAY BEAR WITNESS
TO THOSE I WOULD HELP OF THY LOVE
AND THY WAY OF LIFE.
MAY I DO THY WILL ALWAYS!**

It takes a little humility to say, "I need help," which removes the selfish motive of ego satisfaction. The alcoholic at his core is "selfish," and his choices reflect that. I am living proof of that, having chosen to lie, to write bad checks, and to hurt the people I love, rather than to admit failure and /or disappointment.

I regret those choices every day, and strive to get "out of my own way" in dealing today. "EGO" to me means "easing God out" and I need a higher power to direct my life. It's not easy. The urge to drink has been lifted from me, but it is conditional. I must be honest, humble, and willing to practice the steps, to maintain this lack of urge to drink. **The moment** I forget that I am powerless and selfish at heart – I'll drink again.

Thanks for reading! Thanks, Jimmy for your love.

Your friend, Dad

9TH INNING

"TALENT WINS GAMES,
BUT TEAMWORK AND INTELLIGENCE
WIN CHAMPIONSHIPS."
– Michael Jordan

BOTTOM OF THE NINTH

If you had to make the choice between someone living and someone dying, which would you choose?

- What if that person was your mom, brother, son, sister, wife, or husband?
- What if that person was your best friend?
- What if I told you it was your dad?

Let's just say, for Pete's sake, that it is YOU who has to make the choice. YOU are the one who has to weigh your options. YOU are the one who has to stay up late and think about the outcome. Are you willing to do that for someone you love?

Now, on the flip side, YOU are the one who needs help. Are YOU willing to come full circle and face the facts?

- Would you listen to your mom, dad, brother, sister, friend, wife, or husband?
- Would you be willing to forgive them, if they were willing to help you?
- Would you see the value of them helping you, or would you just take it for granted?
- Would you admit you have a problem in order for anyone to continue helping you?

With those questions come many thoughts and feelings: Where does one draw the line for helping someone else out? With my dad, I really did not know what to do. I loved him, I cared for him, I enjoyed being around him. But as he continued on with his addiction and fell further and further into denial, I could tell that I was no longer helping the cause. I could see that all I was adding was love, and that is powerful, but love was not going to get him help. "Help!" was the cry from his heart, and I had to quit on him physically. I made that choice; I made that decision. I knew that my dad needed to face the consequences on his own; I did not have the financial or emotional resources to help him. But what we did have was a supportive family and friends. That, to me, is what got my dad and me back on our feet. Money cannot buy you love. We did not have a ton of money growing up, but we sure had a ton of love in our family.

When I write this statement, it hits me really hard – I see famous people all the time getting hurt or hurting other people with their addictions. They have all the money in the world; they have all the resources in the world. They have the best doctors, the best lawyers – what appears the best of everything. What I have come to find out as I've grown into my early forties, and my dad into his early sixties, is that none of them have unconditional love. If they do, I do not see it. I see repeat offenders and repeat violators, who always blame someone else for their problems. Unconditional love is why my dad and I are writing this book together, and unconditional love is what got this book in your hands today. It is the answer to all the madness in the world. Love the person for who they are; love them so much that you would go to bat for them, love them so much that it hurts and is a challenge to confront them. Take the first step, tell them you love them unconditionally, and the start of a new game will commence, and you will win that game. I know you will. Dad and I did it, and you can do it as well. You just have to believe in them and them in you. IT WILL HAPPEN, trust us; loving any person unconditionally is well worth it.

The hardest thing to grasp is that you must be willing to lay it on the line. Watching someone you love take his/her life to the depths of addiction is not the greatest roller coaster ride in the park. But sometimes, even great rides have to be shut down for routine maintenance. They need updated information, new wiring, they need new track laid, old rust sanded out, and new primer and paint put on. Then the day comes when the operator is ready for the test run; all is well. Everything passes with flying colors. Opening day, grand opening, or grand re-opening arrives. All the managers and equipment engineers are around taking notes. Sometimes, something comes up that they overlooked or passed in the test run – and they have to shut it down again. People in the park are upset; they'd lined up for hours to get the chance to see and ride it again. More effort and more time are spent on fixing the problem than was never foreseen. Months of planning are down the drain, but while the ride is shut down, the glitch that caused it to malfunction is caught, fixed, and ironed out. You have another run at it. This time, day after day, the roller coaster is functioning correctly – and people are admiring you for having had the vision to shut it down and properly reconcile the problem. The outcome is settled for many years; the roller coaster out lives its life span, and the ride can be enjoyed by everyone.

So as we finish this book, I would like to leave you with this thought. If someone had an addiction problem, would you be willing to quit on him/her in order to get that person back? Would you be willing to shut that person down to fix the problem? Get him/her to the maintenance department? Because my dad and I are not engineers, we are not social workers, or doctors, or priests, but those men and women had to help rebuild us. God will help guide you to the right people, the right programs, and the correct path. But it will boil down to YOU. You have to look the denial right in the face, and ask, *Do I want to be the person I was, before my addiction? Do I want this person with the addiction problem to come back to his or her old form?* It is a choice – so chose wisely and do not be embarrassed to ask for help.

I hope this never happens to you or to your family. If it does, face up to it, make it work, and never give up. I was never educated on alcoholism; I never understood halfway houses or the Prospect House. I never knew what the 12 Steps of A.A. were. But I was educated the hard way; I went through it to learn it. What I hope to pass on to you is the need to get educated on the healing process. Read books, check out Al Anon, and attend A.A. meetings yourself. Talk to your pastor or priest; confront a friend. Tell someone that you need guidance, and without any hesitation the doors of joyfulness will open. Just do not put it off, because whatever you said you are going to do tomorrow is probably what you said you were going to do yesterday. DO IT TODAY. Take action in order to get results.

The genesis of my dad's sobriety for nine years came out of Step 1 of A.A. **We admitted we were powerless over alcohol, that**

our lives had become unmanageable. This statement is the key to starting something tremendous; it is the key that will unlock every door to being sober. Without it, nothing will ever change. Believe me, it works on the addict and the victims. Do not deny it – confront it, and a whole new world of happiness will be available to you and those you love. Do not wait, do it today! This relationship I have with my dad is proof that all things work out in the end, as long as YOU never give up on what is special to you........**Go the Distance.**

On the day before I was going to allow people outside of my family to review this book for the first time, I received the following poem from a dear friend, Marcia. I knew this poem was meant to be in this book. I knew, more importantly, that this poem expressed what my dad gave me, and what I am giving to my child.

PARENT'S PRAYER

*They are little only once, Lord. Grant me the wisdom
and the patience to teach them to follow in Your footsteps
and prepare them for what is to come.*

*They are little only once, Lord. Make me take the time
to play pretend, to read or tell a story, to cuddle.
Don't let me for one minute think anything is more important
than the school play, recital, the big game, fishing
or a quiet walk hand in hand.
All too soon, Lord, they will grow away
and there is no turning back.
Let me have my memories with no regrets.*

*Please help me to be a good parent, Lord.
When I must discipline – let me do it in love, let me be firm,
but fair, let me correct and explain with patience.
They are growing away, Lord.
While I have the chance, let me do my best for them.
For the rest of our lives, please, Lord;
let me be their very best friend.*

POST-GAME NOTES

"DO NOT JUDGE AND YOU WILL NOT BE JUDGED. DO NOT CONDEMN, AND YOU WILL NOT BE CONDEMNED. FORGIVE, AND YOU WILL BE FORGIVEN."
– Luke 6:37

POST-GAME NOTES

The relationship that I have now with my dad is one that will last for eternity, thanks to our willingness to go through the brick wall instead of just stopping and staring at it, and saying, "What should we do next?" It is how we overcame challenges, and how we have developed ourselves, in order to gain extra innings in life. As I look back over the years and realize how far we have come, I can see that love, unconditional love, is what got our relationship back on track. The reason is, *we* forgave each other for our past mistakes, and have focused our attention on the present and on our future together.

Father's Day is but one day a year, but ever since my dad gave up drinking, Father's Day is every day to me. Seeing, hearing, hugging and kissing my dad is the greatest Father's Day gift that a dad can give to a son. I get to see him when I want, and talk to him when I want. I am indebted to the many people, groups, and foundations that have helped develop my dad into the man he is today, and applaud them for giving us many extra innings together. Thanks to them, these next twenty, thirty, thirty-five years with him will not be wasted in regret at not having built our relationship into something we can cherish.

2012 –

2013 –

2014 –

2015 –

2016 –

2017 –

2018 –

2019 – and beyond. The list will go on forever, long after my Dad is gone, because we did something about it. I will pass on very positive thoughts, powerful lessons, and life-changing situations that I experienced with my Dad to my children, family and friends, because I made the decision to go the distance with him. With the years above, I will be able to fill in the blanks with great trips and memories, because we kept the communication lines open. We were willing to put our family first and ourselves second. I *LOVE* him.

As you can tell by the way this book is written, I did almost all of the writing. This book was a very big obstacle for my Dad to talk about, to put together and, most of all, to share with me. But in doing so, we were able to look denial right in the face, and admit that these actions hurt us, our family and our friends. I was very afraid to tell my friends about my dad. I was ashamed of him.

Today, through forgiveness of what transpired, I have grown to be very proud of my dad. I love talking about him, and I love sharing his adversities and his feats with other people. For if I do not share how we achieved it together, how can anyone else see that alcoholism can be overcome? It is being able to share this victory story with another dad, maybe a guy in Arkansas, or maybe to share this story with another son in Alaska, and help him see the way, that motivated us to finish it. Maybe it will be read by someone in a mother/daughter relationship who has been hit with a similar situation, or by a single mom, or by a dad with a child. It is telling people that it is okay to admit that you have a problem; it is okay to be mad, angry, and worried. It is okay to share those thoughts with other people. It is NOT okay to sit back and wait for the outcome. I did that with my dad during my high school years, and through my college and Navy years. I lost contact with high school friends, fraternity brothers and Navy buddies because I was hiding something very deep within me, and I did not want to be judged by them. Those days are long gone for my dad and me.

No matter where my dad is, he now is able to share thoughts and feelings about his alcoholism, and how that led to his suicide attempts, with other families so that this may never happen to them. I see this book as far more than just a bunch of pages bundled together. It is like a diary that was kept locked up in a time capsule for future fathers and sons, and mothers and daughters, to open and learn something about a piece of personal history. But history is about the past, something long gone. This book that we both put together is more about doing something in the present in order to have a future together, so that history can be re-written for the better.

Today is June 29, 2011. Tomorrow, I have to call the publishing company to go over the editing of the book before it goes into print. There is one last item that I need to share with you, reader, on why my father's and my relationship continues to flourish. Just two weeks ago, I got a hold of the Prospect House. I explained to them that my dad and I had written a book about our highs and lows. With that, they invited my dad and me to their yearly picnic. I took them up on the invitation, and drove to Cincinnati from Carmel, Indiana. I met my dad at the Holiday Inn just north of Cincinnati and we drove over to Sharon Woods Park together as a team. As we pulled in, my dad said that he had to work the picnic; to help serve food, to man the grill, to greet people, and to do everything he could to make other alcoholics and their families feel welcome to a very special place in his heart, and in theirs. We parked the car and within five minutes a big, burly man yelled "Jim!"

My dad turned and sure enough, even ten years later, my dad remembered this man's name. They hugged, they talked, and he introduced him to me. My dad had a huge smile on his face.

When we walked down the hill five minutes later, another man came up and said, "Jim!" He too gave my dad a huge hug, and Dad introduced me to him. Five minutes later it happened again, then again, and again. My dad was on cloud nine; he was tearing up with joy, not because of the fact that they knew his name, but because he was happy to be there among the men who had changed his life. He was happy that I was there with him, he was happy that the picnic was so successful; 3,000 men with their families were there that day. It was a victory celebration for all who were there. They will celebrate again in 2012, 2013, and 2014, and my dad and I will be there.

We sat down at the lunch table and the president came over and hugged him, the cook, "Tweety," came over and hugged him, his mentor hugged him, and even his counselor was put on the phone to talk to my dad. Other men who never knew him talked to him, and he to them. It was like he had been there this whole time. Love, happiness, appreciation, forgiveness, and bonding went on in the two-plus hours we were there. Like I said earlier in the book, A.A. is my dad's league of sober men and that day, and all the days leading to the future, are what give my dad and me the strength to carry out his mission. I had never seen my dad so delighted to be a part of something over the past few years, outside of our family. This book was "meant to be" for both of us, because I've seen how writing it has opened up additional doors that he and I had closed.

It was very troublesome for my dad to write this book; he admitted to me that he would write two or three pages, then he would just begin to cry and he would throw them out. I came over to his house expecting him to have written a few chapters, and all I got was an outline. But that day at the picnic put everything that he and I had worked on into fresh perspective for us. It is the fact that my dad is alive, my dad is sober, my dad has a family and that he and I are able to continue to *Go the Distance* for each other, that matters the most.

    – Jim Serger Jr.

Recommended Reading

1. *Understanding the Twelve Steps* by Terence T. Gorski
2. *Extreme Dreams Depend on Teams* by Pat Williams
3. *Today Matters* by John C. Maxwell
4. *1% Solution for Work and Life* by Tom Connellan
5. *Mr. Little John's Secrets to A Lifetime of Success* by Pat Williams
6. *The Fred Factor* by Mark Sanborn
7. *The Warrior Within* by Pat Williams
8. *Winning With People* by John C Maxwell
9. *Think Like a Champion* by Donald J. Trump
10. *What Are You Living For?* by Pat Williams
11. *Bear Bryant on Leadership* by Pat Williams

About the Authors

JIM, SENIOR

Selected by Philadelphia Phillies out of high school; graduated from the University of Cincinnati having played third base on the baseball team, Theta Chi fraternity member. He worked in sales all his life, having lived a few years in Louisville, Kentucky and Columbus, Indiana. He raised his family for 30 years in Anderson Township in Cincinnati, Ohio. Jim was a youth baseball head coach for 14 years, and is the proud father of two sons. He has a best friend, Marilyn, who is also his wife. His greatest accomplishment in life was being welcomed back into a family that loves him, for being himself. Jim loves the Cincinnati Bearcats programs, and the Cincinnati Reds. Jim has given speeches on the severity of alcoholism at the Hamilton County Jail in Cincinnati a few times. Jim is a loving grandpa, and is a proud father-in-law. Jim loves being surrounded by lifelong friends and loves to create new ones. Jim currently lives in New Richmond, Ohio.

JIM JUNIOR

Graduated from the University of Cincinnati; Delta Tau Delta Fraternity member. He served four years in the U.S. Navy. He lived in Japan for four years; served on board the *USS Independence* CV-62. Jim loves to travel, and has been to 23 states and 13 countries. Jim backpacked through Asia; climbed Mt. Fuji, and is an avid sports fan. Jim loves to read, and in 2010, read 71 books. He has worked at Home City Ice since getting out of the Navy 15 years ago. Jim loves his life and his family very much. He and his loving wife, Tarla, have an adorable six-year-old girl named Maggie. Jim Jr. is very proud of his family name, and would share this or any other story about his family, because he loves them unconditionally and is proud of them all for overcoming adversity. They currently live in Carmel, Indiana.

You can visit our website, www.JimSerger.com

Or contact us at the following emails.
To contact Jim Jr.: Jim@jimserger.com
To contact Big Jim: Bigjim@jimserger.com

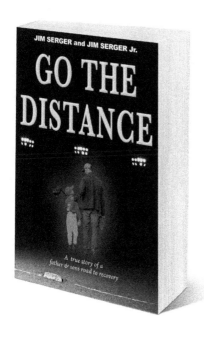

How can you use this book?

Motivate

Educate

Thank

Inspire

Promote

Connect

Why have a custom version of *Go The Distance*?

- Build personal bonds with customers, prospects, employees, donors, and key constituencies
- Develop a long-lasting reminder of your event, milestone, or celebration
- Provide a keepsake that inspires change in behavior and change in lives
- Deliver the ultimate "thank you" gift that remains on coffee tables and bookshelves
- Generate the "wow" factor

Books are thoughtful gifts that provide a genuine sentiment that other promotional items cannot express. They promote employee discussions and interaction, reinforce an event's meaning or location, and they make a lasting impression. Use your book to say "Thank You" and show people that you care.